REFLEXIVE INQUIRY

Other titles in the
Systemic Thinking and Practice Series
edited by David Campbell & Ros Draper
published and distributed by Karnac

Credit Card orders, Tel: +44 (0) 20-8969-4454; Fax: +44 (0) 20-8969-5585
Email: shop@karnacbooks.com

REFLEXIVE INQUIRY

A Framework for Consultancy Practice

by

Christine Oliver

Foreword by

Sheila McNamee

Systemic Thinking and Practice Series

Series Editors
David Campbell & Ros Draper

KARNAC
LONDON   NEW YORK

Published in 2005 by
Karnac (Books) Ltd.
6 Pembroke Buildings, London NW10 6RE

British Library Cataloguing in Publication Data

A C.I.P. for this book is available from the British Library

ISBN 1 85575 358 8

Edited, designed, and produced by The Studio Publishing Services Ltd, Exeter EX4 8JN

Printed in Great Britain

www.karnacbooks.com

CONTENTS

SERIES EDITORS' FOREWORD

At a time when an increasing number of models and approaches to organizational work claim some connection to systemic thinking, it is very helpful to find a book that brings many conceptual strands together. As in any field, boundaries between theoretical models are essential at an early stage of development, but then they soon prevent dialogue between competing models. Christine Oliver's book opens up a dialogue by critiquing models such as Appreciative Inquiry (AI); the Coordinated Management of Meaning (CMM); and the domains model. Gradually she weaves these ideas together to form her own integrative model that she calls Reflexive Inquiry (RI).

Another feature of many organizational books is their emphasis on practical solutions at the expense of theoretical explanation, however Oliver has produced very strong, and very clear, theoretical arguments for the work she is doing, all of which helps the reader take away deeper understanding as well as practical suggestions for work with organizations. The five principles underpinning her model are discussed methodically in two case studies to enable the reader to understand how the model can be put into action.

One of the most interesting aspects of this innovative book is a chapter about research. This sets out to explain how the RI model can be adapted to research so that consultants can continue to evaluate their work and learn from the process. The book is carefully constructed and extremely well argued, and we think these ideas are a serious contribution to the development of the field of organizational work.

David Campbell
Ros Draper
London, July 2005

ABOUT THE AUTHOR

Christine Oliver has an MSc in Social Policy from the LSE and works as an organizational consultant, systemic psychotherapist, and teacher and trainer in psychotherapy and organizational studies at KCC Foundation and at Queen Mary College, London. She is the author/co-author of a number of journal papers and book chapters. In a recent book, *Complexity, Relationships and Strange Loops: A Reflexive Practice Guide* (2003) with co-authors Herasymowych and Senko, she advocated reflexivity as essential for building effective relational practices amongst organizational members. In this book, reflexivity is treated as a core practice for consultants in their work with organizations.

FOREWORD

Organizations are part of our lives. They add significantly to our relationships, our competence, and our passions. They also add significantly to our anxiety, our sense of deficiency, and our stress. We love them and we hate them. We cannot live with them and we cannot live without them. Our organizational lives are complex, compelling, and critical to who we are and how we live.

Chris Oliver's book, *Reflexive Inquiry: A Framework for Consultancy Practice*, offers a way for us, as organizational members and consultants, to handle the tensions of a life immersed in organizational relations, structures, rules, policies, and procedures. This book provides us with an array of practices we might use with client systems seeking development while avoiding the urge to prescribe a *new* method for consultancy. Oliver invites us to ask how we can remain present in the dialogical tension of organizational life. She provokes us to consider how we can introduce transformation in meaning and action in the face of heated conflict and personal mistrust. Ultimately, this book positions us to wonder if, in our work as consultants, we have methods for helping organizational members *go on together* (Wittgenstein, 1953) in ways that do not silence, oppress, marginalize, or ignore the multiple beliefs, ethics, and values circulating within any given organization. As Oliver makes clear in her opening words, her aim is to "help organizations create coherence between their vision, strategy and action". But to do so, she reminds us, requires that our consultancy practices remain coherent not only to our clients but to us, as professionals, as well.

Rather than determining a strict structure for organizational consultancy, Oliver provides a generative template within which one can improvise and construct ever-new modes of dialogue. She does so by drawing on a range of practices emanating from a constructionist orientation: systemic family therapy (Selvini, Cecchin, Prata, & Boscolo, 1978), the coordinated management of meaning theory (Cronen, Johnson, & Lannamann, 1982; Pearce, 1989), and appreciative inquiry (Cooperrider, 1998). As elaborations of social constructionist discourse, each of these specific modes of inquiry shares the understanding that we create the realities within which we live *together* in our moment to moment interactions with each other. These interactions, in turn, take place within localized traditions that are historically and culturally situated. What becomes central here is *what* people do together rather than what motivates them to act. To make sense at all requires that we look at the interactive practices (i.e., communication) of people in relation.

By emphasizing communication processes within organizations, Oliver proposes reflexive inquiry as our main consultancy tool. We become interested to connect members' *self examinations* of their feelings, thoughts, and actions with their *relational reflections*. Thus, Oliver provides us with tools for initiating generative dialogues among organizational members. The dialogues are generative to the extent that they invite participants to inquire about the ways in which their actions coordinate with the actions of others to create the culture of their organization. Our focus is fully centred on communication practices. Oliver is interested in inviting her organizational clients into a stance that allows them to critically assess and explore their own actions. This stance is familiar to anyone working within a postmodern sensibility and is commonly referred to as self reflexivity. However, Oliver takes the reflexive stance one step further by inviting organizational members to move beyond mere self examination to *relational and cultural exploration*. Specifically, her template for reflexive inquiry invites participants within an organization to reflect on the relational nature of their actions: the relational networks that grant them coherence and vitality and the way in which they are transformed when introduced into different relational networks (such as their organization). This relational examination invites members to acknowledge the necessity of each other in crafting *coherent* working systems.

While any one of the orientations she draws on (systemic therapy, the coordinated management of meaning theory, and appreciative inquiry), alone, can and has been used to consult organizations, the hybrid that Oliver presents in this volume speaks to her theme of *coherence*. She acknowledges the reflexive stance as the key to transformation. And, in using this stance as an organizing template, she invites us as consultants to play with the tools and principles she describes. Her integrative resources for consultancy offer opportunities for new organizational conversations in a way that moves beyond the limits of any one mode. For example, in Oliver's hands, appreciative inquiry expands to embrace critical appreciation and appreciative criticism. In doing so, the complexity of organizational life is not dismissed in favour of voicing only the positive aspects of the organization.

Oliver ends this volume articulating, "Dialogue processes can be designed to enhance coherence but we always need to be alert to the situational requirements of the complex moment". What I find most appealing about this volume is the way Oliver has remained alert to the complexity of the moment. She has created a flexible and fluid stance toward organizational change. She encourages us to wonder how we might, as consultants, prepare ourselves to work with organizational members in such a way that they reflexively entertain the processes by which they make organizational meanings together. Yet, consistent with the constructionist mantra that "there is no constructionist technique", she invites her reader into a constructionist understanding of meaning-making and then proceeds to creatively integrate very different elaborations of this sensibility into an open and pliable consultancy structure. Oliver, clearly at home with theory and broad philosophical issues, introduces us to practical, collaborative resources for consultancy. These resources are based on her work with organizations and clearly demonstrate the sort of agility she is advocating and how reflexive inquiry assists us in developing this sort of agility.

In her integrative work, she has devised a model that holds together by virtue of its reflexive stance. As she claims, ". . . consciousness about the patterns of feeling, meaning and action that we, and others, are experiencing in a relational system are central to effective organizational development". To that end, she sets herself the task of elaborating a set of principles and tools that flexibly invite respect and curiosity for difference, and it is this respect and curiosity that allows for coordination of diversity so that organizational members can collaboratively construct something viable together. In her detailed case illustrations we see the members of organizations collaborating in their own transformation. In other models of organizational change, we see the consultants *directing* organizational members towards transformation. Oliver has centralized the communication process and participants' reflexive curiosity about that process. Attending to our processes of relating—that is, how we are connecting and communicating with each other—is where organizational transformation occurs.

It was a joy for me personally to read this volume. I felt as if I was reading a history of my own professional trajectory: the coordinated management of meaning theory, systemic family therapy, therapy and consultation as social construction, the adoption of an appreciative stance. But rather than see each move as an improvement on what has come before, I see each of these modes of inquiry as a variation on a theme. Oliver has struck a chord in identifying reflexive inquiry as the centerpiece of our work. When we invite our clients (as well as ourselves) into the sort of *relational* examination that reflexive inquiry spawns, we give full attention to the communication practices that create our identities, our organizations, and our lives. I am sure this volume will be rich with resources for us all.

Sheila McNamee
Professor of Communication
University of New Hampshire
Durham, New Hampshire, USA

Co-Founder and Board Member, The Taos Institute

Introduction

As an organizational consultant drawing on systemic traditions, I aspire to help organizations create coherence between their vision, strategy, and action. By the same token, coherence is an important context for my own practice. I find myself comparing, connecting, and distinguishing my experiences as a consultant, moving between frames, tools, and practices and back again and developing a thread of narrative as I go. This book on reflexive inquiry (RI) represents an attempt to articulate that narrative and will hold value in so far as it can inspire others to act productively in specific situated moments. I am grateful for the opportunity to make a pattern of my experience. In taking up this opportunity, my own practice, at least, has developed.

Reflecting on the theme of coherence, I realize the usefulness of experiences of incoherence to my own learning as a practitioner in organizational contexts. I have attempted to cultivate the ability to notice points of disconnection and to connect them to wider contexts that help disconnection to make sense. This consciousness has facilitated the potential for new frames and tools, providing, in turn, contexts for future dissonances. My work with appreciative inquiry (AI) is an example where an experience of incoherence has been fruitful in helping me challenge and change my frames and practices to construct (from where I stand) a more coherent pattern. I am grateful to writers and practitioners of AI who have inspired these developments (Anderson et al., 2001; Barge & Oliver, 2003; Cooperrider, 1998; Cooperrider & Whitney, 1999).

AI has become a prevalent consultancy methodology discourse for working with organizational change and, for some, has become aligned with systemic practice (Anderson et al,, 2001). The impetus for this book comes from both the practical development of this methodology in my work as a consultant, and the translation of that work in teaching and writing contexts—teaching on the MSc in Systemic Organization and Management at Kensington Consultation Centre, London, writing various papers for conferences and publication (Barge & Oliver, 2003) and two recent chapters on AI in edited books (Oliver & Barge, 2002, Oliver, 2005). An increasing need to develop AI methodology to fit the contexts I work in helped me to understand some theoretical (and practical) disconnections implicit in the methodology itself. I moved through various representations (for example, Critical Appreciative Inquiry, Oliver, 2005) to a position of thinking that reflexive inquiry could provide the possibility of both transcending the polarization of *positive* and *negative* embedded in appreciative inquiry and incorporating something of its value. Thus, RI is employed as a set of principles and tools in presenting my particular approach to consultancy in working with organizational development.

This approach is inspired by systemic practice in psychotherapy and organizational studies. While a systemic account encourages the practitioner to engage with and develop the complexity of life and *not marry one's hypothesis*, I detect a discomfort in some representations of systemic thought with the critical and the decisive voice, privileging the empowerment of the voice of the other in a way that can create systemic imbalance (e.g. see Anderson et al, 2001). My own 1996 paper, "Systemic eloquence", was an attempt to posit reflexivity as the core practice, with systemic eloquence as the space in which situated decisions could be made about the appropriate form of communication required, whether appreciative, challenging, critical, decisive, supportive, or inquiring. My thinking now is that paper did not go far enough in making a case for reflexivity as a core practice. This book offers more of a basis for that position by connecting a related set of principles to a repertoire of practice.

In developing the methodology of RI, I am offering models and tools constituting *practical theory* in my work with organizations. In using the term practical theory I am moving away from the traditional academic dualism separating theoretical constructs from their applications. Instead, I am aiming to demonstrate the opportunities for organization development and learning that arise from examples of RI theory-in-practice.

In Part I of the book the RI frame is set out. Five core principles are offered to set a theoretical and ethical context for the tools required for constructing and coordinating conversation that can be said to make up RI practice.

In Part II, these principles and tools come to life when enacted in organizational and community development contexts. Work described is that undertaken with a religious community and in a non-governmental organization (NGO), where the development of reflexive practice became vital for existence. All organizations embody unique patterns of meaning and action, thus the learning from work with one can never be translated "lock stock and barrel". However, the methodologies and tools that are set out in Part I are shown in action in the case studies. This demonstrates the potential of these tools to construct new patterns of feeling, meaning, and action that provide scope for ways forward in complex, uncomfortable, and sometimes stuck situations.

Part III draws out some implications of the principles, arguments, models, and tools presented for undertaking research. It is argued that RI provides unique possibilities for research. A case example is offered that shows a rich connection between consultancy and research processes.

Part IV concludes, and looks at the potential for future development. In particular, it shares recent ideas in development about looped patterns in communication.

Christine Oliver
September 2005

PART I

FRAMES AND TOOLS

CHAPTER ONE

Reflexive inquiry principles for consultancy practice

I n this chapter the five RI principles that can be employed in specific, local, situated moments and episodes of organizational practice are defined and illustrated. I hope to show the liberating power of an RI orientation in enabling the development of purpose, choice, and agency in the organizational patterns that, with others, we create. In this, the development of consciousness, appreciation, and critique of relational dynamics and their effects will be encouraged, not as an end in itself but as an essential component of what could be called *organizational intelligence*.

RI rests on the assumption that consciousness about the patterns of feeling, meaning and action that we, and others, are experiencing in a relational system is central to effective organizational development. This critical consciousness is predicated on an appreciation that identities, relationships, and cultural practices are interconnected to our and others' actions. When we practise reflexivity we make *choices* about how we will think and act. We become *responsible* and *accountable* for our choices, our actions, and our contributions to a relational system.

RI is positioned here as valuable to both process and product in organizational development (OD) initiatives. Peck, in an introductory book on OD in the NHS (2005), presents OD as developing coherence between the organization, its members, and its environment. He points out that the history of OD has differently emphasized at different points, processes, structures, people, and culture in its attempts to improve organizational performance. He proposes the value of an integrated approach but, in particular, argues that OD initiatives should be judged on whether they enhance the potential of the *changing* organization as opposed to the *changed* organization. He suggests that the *changing* organization builds into its structures, processes, and culture, ways of examining itself. Thus, he advocates a continual reflexivity.

A focus on reflexivity has been a thread in my previous writings, particularly in the paper "Systemic eloquence" (Oliver, 1996), which built on Pearce's distinction between social and rhetorical eloquence (Pearce, 1989). Social eloquence was defined as a set of communication abilities privileging the *second person*, facilitating openness to the other. Rhetorical eloquence, on the other hand, privileged the first person and included abilities such as persuasion. "Systemic eloquence", foregrounding the moral actor, attempted to highlight how systemic work requires both for an integrated reflexive practice. This book develops the account of "Systemic eloquence" by drawing on more abstracted theoretical principles for its inspiration for reflexive practice. Within that account, it opens up and details the reflexive space in acts and patterns of communication.

The five principles that constitute RI position us reflexively in relationship to ourselves, others, and the patterns and stories that we make (Oliver, Herasymowych, & Senko, 2003, Pearce, 1994). The notion of principle is being used here as a higher order context that frames meaning and guides action. These principles are *systemic*, *constructionist*, *critical*, *appreciative*, and *complex*. While it could be argued that each principle runs through all five, they are highlighted individually to distinguish the value of each one as a lens.

Systemic principle

- Patterns of connection.
- Patterns lived and stories told.

- Patterns make sense when we widen the context.
- We are not outside the pattern.

Patterns of connection

At the heart of a systemic orientation to practice is an interest in patterns of connection (Bateson, 1972). We look for patterns in how people feel, how they make meaning and how they act, and in the interplay between them. The word pattern can be hard to grasp. The word is used here to mean forms of feeling, thinking, and action that repeat over time, that become embedded as stories in organizational culture, relationships, and identities (see Table 1).

For instance, a manager, in the context of staff complaint, might react in an *authoritarian* way, which has the effect of stifling voices of staff that in turn encourages complaint, and so on. The identity and relational positions available to participants in this pattern become limiting and other forms of communication are discouraged, making a cultural pattern of poor accountability, underdeveloped

Table 1. Pattern of connection embedded in organizational stories

Type of communication	Description
Organisational culture stories	Explicit and implicit stories about the ways things can and should be done, e.g., *authoritarian decision-making*
Relational stories	Stories of who we are, can be, and should be in relationship, e.g., *I can veto your decisions*
Identity stories	Stories of who an individual is, can and should be, e.g., *I am a decision-maker*
Episode of communication	Boundaried sequence of communications, e.g., *a meeting*
Pattern of connection	Made up of feeling, meaning, and action, e.g., *feel irritated, interpret it as being about not having power, take action by complaining*

responsibility, and stifled agency and initiative, which in turn shapes ongoing communication patterns.

Patterns lived and stories told

The use of the word *story* has a particular place of significance within a systemic orientation in the sense that we create accounts about our organizational behaviour patterns that take the form of a story, containing character, relationship, plot, emotion, and meaning (Pearce, 1994).[1] Our stories can never articulate the richness of the patterns that we live. In systemic practice we are mindful of the stories we hear and are interested in how they have been constructed and what possibilities for action they construct in organizational life. For instance, the manager might tell the story that his staff don't take sufficient initiative, and may not see how his own patterns lived and stories told might contribute to cultural stories that set a context for such a staff response. Two particular areas of interest for a consultant might be whether patterns and stories are either connected through sameness or through difference. If they are too similar, there is a tendency for organizational members to impose their own experience on others as if it represents a totalizing truth. If they are too different, organizational members may experience incoherence and lack of trust in organizational relationships, processes, and structures.

It is important to be mindful of the stories we tell as consultants, and take seriously how they might shape the organizational realities we are responsible for influencing. For instance, our stories about power and how the diversity of voices in organizational life should be encouraged or limited will affect our interventions.

In examining and creating stories, a special interest is taken in the possibilities and constraints embedded in language. The use of a word can be seen as a moral and political act in that the ways we use language shape possibilities for agency and contribution, enabling or disabling meaningful and purposeful participation in organizational life. If a member of staff repeatedly states, *my voice is not heard* he may, perhaps, encourage a pattern of interaction, which reinforces that story. This may be because the repetitiveness of the claim, almost irrespective of its validity, constrains progress, in that the manager, as audience to the story, is positioned as ineffective. This lack of agency may lead to a sense of stuckness, frustration, and low morale. In these circumstances the meaning of the message will possibly be interpreted as *complaint*, and energy to respond to the claim is diminished. In turn this may lead to the manager resorting to structural power and an *authoritarian* response. By contrast, if the member of staff had expressed a concern about a pattern in which he found it difficult to take initiative, he might be taking some responsibility for the pattern, reframing meaning (Boscolo, Cecchin, Hoffman, & Penn, 1987) and arguably opening up possibilities for change. Similarly, if the manager was able to find a more creative interpretation of the communication, such as *requesting support* rather than *complaint*, he may find himself more able to transcend the pattern.

Patterns make sense when we widen the context

When we examine an individual action and seek explanation for why it has occurred, our resources are limited unless we can explore how that action is embedded in a larger pattern of experiences and stories (Shotter, 1993). We can resort to explanations such as, *he is a difficult person*, or *they are a lazy team*, but such explanations offer limited possibilities for action if they fix the part while leaving the whole unattended (Oliver & Lang, 1994). While a *difficult person* or a *lazy team* can be challenged or encouraged, if the behaviour of the part is understood in the context of the whole, the possibilities for action are increased. For instance, one might ask, how has the *lazy team* been constructed? What part does management initiative play in encouraging or discouraging a *lazy team*? We can be helped to make sense of the wider context through an appreciation of the significance of language and how it shapes possibilities.

We are not outside the pattern

The systemic tradition supports the view that our observations of the system affect the system (Boscolo, Cecchin, Hoffman, & Penn, 1987). By extension, a moral position is implied here of cultivating awareness of the contribution one might be making to the patterns and processes of which one is a part. Thus, the manager, faced with unwanted behaviour from a staff member, might ask himself: *what am I doing to invite certain behaviours from the staff member and constrain others?*

Constructionist principle

- Communication is action.
- Context constructs communication and communication constructs context.
- Person position is an element of a story.
- Stories express a moral force.

Communication is action

For the social constructionist, like the systemic practitioner, there is a concern and interest in the detail of language (verbal and non-verbal) and in the opportunities and constraints created by communication for the organizational system (Burr, 1995; Campbell, 2000; Gergen, 1989; Pearce, 1989). The position is taken that our communication makes our social realities—our powers to act, participate, take up positions, and make particular contributions. The social constructionist is concerned to employ a reflexive responsibility for the identities, relationships, and cultures that we create through the ways we communicate. This requires cultivating consciousness about our behaviour and using that consciousness to develop action that is more sensitive to the needs of the situation. The usefulness of this frame for the consultant is in the idea that the power to make change is found in conversation. Thus, an important task of the consultant becomes the structuring of effective, reflexive dialogue. This claim will become clearer when we examine the relationship between context and communication.

Context constructs communication and communication constructs context

The coordinated management of meaning (CMM) contextual framework of Cronen & Pearce (1985) has enriched social constructionist organizational (and therapeutic) practice (Oliver, 1992, 1996). They have imbued the word context with complex but practical significance, providing a means, with their model of *layers of context*, to make sense of the relationship between feeling, meaning and action in patterns lived and stories told. They have offered us *places to look* in patterns and stories that help us to make sense of, and act within, complex organizational systems. They are interested in the relationship between layers of context such as organizational culture, relationship, identity, role, task, and episode and invite us to invoke any other context that might be meaningful in a particular situation, e.g., a leadership discourse in an organization or, more personally, where appropriate, family patterns (see Figure 1).

When the notion of context is invoked, we can ask how contextual stories influence meaning and action in an episode of communication. The communication illustrated above, between the manager and staff member, is shaped (from the manager's position) by the hierarchy of contextual stories that exert an influence in the moment that the interpretation of the communication is made. This process is described as an *interpretive act*, reframing Cronen and Pearce's original *speech act* (1985), to convey that one's interpretations have a powerful influence in shaping the next action but this influence is not inevitable. For Cronen and Pearce, the *speech act* was defined as the relational meaning of a message, interpreted by the receiver of a communication, embedded within a hierarchy of meanings. In redefining the *speech act* as the *interpretive act*, the

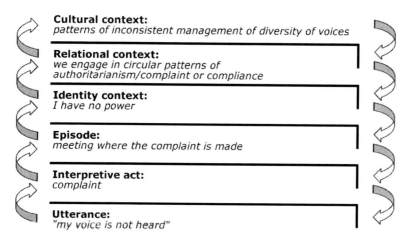

Figure 1.   Contextual and implicative force in patterns of communication

interpretive dimension of meaning-making is highlighted as a moral choice with moral consequences and the responsibility for the interpretation is located in the individual.[2]

We do have a choice, though we sometimes act as if we do not. The influence of these contextual stories, including that of the *interpretive act*, cascading downwards, has been described (Cronen & Pearce, 1985) as *contextual force*. Each contextual story makes sense within the context above. As an illustration of this, the relational context in the example makes sense within the cultural context. Simultaneously, the communication exerts an upward influence on the hierarchy of contexts, reinforcing or reshaping the stories at each contextual level as a consequence of the communication episode-in-progress. The influence of the emergent episode, filtering upwards, has been described as *implicative force*. In the example, if the manager had interpreted the utterance of the staff member in another way, as, for instance, a *request for help*, the communication stemming from this interpretation might serve to challenge the relational context of *authoritarianism/complaint* or *compliance* and if this kind of communication could be consistently made, ultimately the cultural context of *inconsistent management* might change.

This device of levels of context facilitates story-making for the consultant in the way it helps him or her to develop a (speculative) narrative of patterns and stories and the relationships between them. Within this tradition, this process is called hypothesizing. It alerts us to looking for particular elements in stories; for example, *person position* and *subject position* (see below), and the strength of influence of stories at particular levels, both for those we are working with and for ourselves.

Person position as an element of a story

We use language in organizations to allocate *person position* in the ways we use the words *I, we, you, he, she, it, them*, and *us*. These patterns are both telling and consequential in the way that they shape meaning. Moreover, a constructionist orientation also encourages us to see how such usage of words creates our patterns of relating, particularly when their usage is outside our consciousness (Harre & Langenhove, 1999).

In our example, one might hypothesize that the staff member and the manager participate in a cultural language game of *us and them*. It would be interesting to note how the words *I* and *we* are used in connection with expressions of initiative and forms of participation. Within this example, both staff member and manager are positioning the other as *not like me*. Consequently each may feel alienated, having been *positioned* in an adversarial role.

Stories express a moral force

As has been implied, the use of *person position* provides an example of how the detail of language has moral effects (Harre & Langenhove, 1999, Pearce, 1994). In the same way, the small words we use in sentences such as *can*, *should*, and *must* invoke a sense of the moral force of a story. They indicate the operation of tacit *rules* in our interpretations of communication and the actions that follow them. In the example above, the staff member is, perhaps, speaking from a position of *I can't influence* and in so doing, offers the manager the *subject position* (experience of self) of actor and himself the subject position of *acted upon*. The manager may be taking up a moral position (informed by his own mix of cultural, organizational, family, relational, and identity stories of significance) from which the rule emerges: *I must keep tight control or nothing would happen*. It is interesting to hypothesize about where such *rules of obligation and entitlement* might come from (for instance, the manager may have experienced in previous contexts of influence that he became anxious in the face of a lack of control from others); what part they play in the mix of bigger contextual stories (for instance, the senior management team may take a more *laissez faire* attitude than he feels comfortable with); what particular contexts have the strongest force in making them meaningful (for instance, this team may have worked with a previous manager whom they idealized and this manager, misguidedly, may be trying to prove his effectiveness); and where there are points of leverage for development (a strong relationship with one member of staff may allow direct, frank, and reflexive discussion about the tensions in the team). A focus on these elements of a story gets us to the heart of the moral and emotional dimensions of organizational patterns. We become connected to where people feel most constrained and most energized.

Critical principle

- Power is a legitimate and desirable focus for inquiry.
- Meaning is subject to inquiry and challenge.
- Second and third order critique facilitate evaluation.
- Critical consciousness is an aspiration.

Power is a legitimate and desirable focus for inquiry

In the world of critical theory, power is privileged as a focus (Alvesson & Deetz, 2000). The critical analyst sets out to make the construction and enactment of power visible, through inquiry and sense-making. The critical literature, however, shows a tendency to present motivation as self-interested and power hungry (Alvesson & Skoldberg, 2000). RI would, instead, encourage a view that motivation is complex and that we engage in ways that maintain, develop, or challenge our (and others') stories. In these terms, it is seen as legitimate and desirable to explore how we use our voices and positions and the consequences of that use. The interest is in how organizational members can speak accountably but with appropriate authority. Our powers to participate in meaning and decision-making are constructed by and construct organizational discourse. Organizational discourse could be said to be a collective noun for the patterns of connection between organizational culture, relationship, and identity stories. Hierarchical position is relevant in this analysis as it confers and constrains such possibilities. However, RI is interested in the patterns and stories in which hierarchical position is embedded rather than in the objectification of such positions.

Meaning is subject to inquiry and challenge

As illustrated above, we are invited or pressured into particular experiences of self or *subject positions* in relationships. The part we are offered in the organizational discourse, through our participation in cultural and relational patterns, may or may not be desirable. We do not have to take up these invitations to participate, but choosing not to take up a *subject position offered* in a pattern, requires *critical reflexive skills* and the ability to act, when appropriate, counter-intuitively. For instance, both manager and staff member may experience themselves as *without power and undermined*. If one or both were able to take a counter-intuitive position of a strong voice and speak about their experience and invite the other to speak about theirs, the experience of self might change. Consciousness, inquiry, and challenge about the assumptions, relational and subject positions we ourselves take up and offer to others, may encourage an ability to reflect on a pattern where it is important to do so and examine it for its usefulness and fit.

The commitment to inquiry and challenge requires an openness to learn, preparedness to change and a curiosity about the experience of others, positioning self and other as human and vulnerable (Buber, 1970). It requires a kind of humility about one's own position and a sense of obligation to provide accounts to others about our experience and understanding.

Second and third order critique facilitate evaluation

The notion of contextual levels of critique represents a challenge to the position taken by appreciative inquiry (AI) that critique in itself is problematic (Anderson et al., 2001). In *The Appreciative Organization* we are warned against *evaluation* and instead invited to *valuate*. Valuation through affirming others is seen as preferable to evaluation, which is associated with blame, the seeking out of what is wrong or problematic. It is proposed here that this antipathy towards so called *problem talk* from AI methodology is an insufficiently complex response, predicated on an assumption of first order critique. In RI, second and third order critique would usually be more generative, although first order critique is not always inappropriate. There are contexts in which it might be clarifying to allocate responsibility for an action. These levels are defined in the following way:

First order critique: a non-systemic position where the explanation (cause or blame) for a state of affairs is outside the self; e.g., a staff member making the statement, *it is the fault of management*.

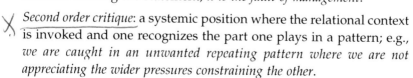

Second order critique: a systemic position where the relational context is invoked and one recognizes the part one plays in a pattern; e.g., *we are caught in an unwanted repeating pattern where we are not appreciating the wider pressures constraining the other*.

Third order critique: a systemic position where the organizational cultural context is invoked and one recognizes one's contribution to that culture; e.g., *the culture is one of inconsistent messages around participation—I need to comment on the cultural pattern and behave consistently myself.*[3]

The development of critical consciousness should facilitate reflexive critique of the system by the system. In my experience, such discussions in organizations are often managed in an unbalanced way through avoidance, control, blame or lack of sensitivity to the complexity of motivation in the system. However, a critical approach as described should allow for the opportunity to bring power to the forefront of participants' consciousness and a challenge to naïve and simplistic stories of equality and hierarchy, while maintaining systemic integrity.

Critical consciousness is an aspiration

When we participate in a communication pattern, we, with others, are participating in a process of meaning-making and decision-making that often feels *natural* and *spontaneous* in its flow, especially when there is an experience of familiarity in the patterns that we make. A key point to convey is that while those familiar patterns can help the organization in its smooth running, they can also constrain creativity and make for stuckness in the flow of productivity. It is suggested that the development of reflexive positioning facilitates organizational production in the ways that it encourages mindfulness in communication about the multiplicity of contexts we are acting out of and into. In calling such mindfulness *critical consciousness*, attention is drawn to the interpretive act and the opportunities it provides for reflection and reflexivity.

Critical consciousness and the interpretive act

The *interpretive act* is broken down into three parts: feeling, interpretation, and action (see Figure 2). This is not to suggest that these are separate dimensions of a response in any crude linear sense, but only that they are useful lenses through which to examine the observations, interpretations, and choices one makes in a commu-

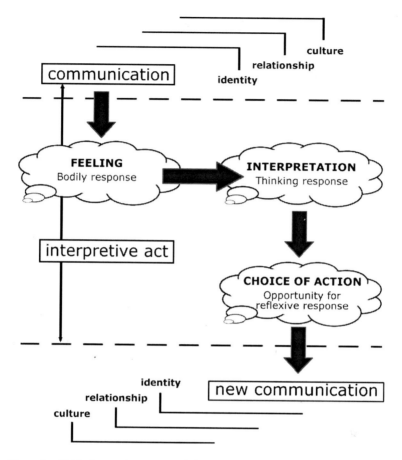

Figure 2. Critical consciousness and the interpretive act in communication

nicative episode. Through amplifying the detail of the *interpretive act* in this way the potential for *reflexive evaluation* is increased, when one can become more conscious of the partiality and multiplicity of possibilities for interpretation and action.

Feeling (bodily response): at the point of receiving a communication, we are helped by our senses to read it. We see, hear, touch and feel what is communicated; we experience sensory and emotional responses. These responses are coloured by the contexts of past experience, cultural and relational contexts, and the environmental context of communication. They are inevitably partial, both in the sense that we can never notice all there is to be noticed and in the sense that our experiences (patterns lived) can only provide us with a partial lens. In our example, the manager may feel a defensive reaction in his body and feel the need to act on it to protect himself—this may be shown in non-verbal clues such as body language and eye contact.

Interpretation (thinking response): our feeling contributes to meaning-making at the interpretive level. In addition, our life experience (patterns lived) and the stories we tell ourselves about those experiences tend to create habitual *rules for interpretation*,[4] which we draw on in communicative processes. However, we can exercise conscious choice in interpreting and reflecting on our interpretations. We can frame the same episode of communication in many different ways, thereby unpacking the multiplicity of meanings that have potentially been conveyed. In fact, an important reflexive ability could be said to be that of engaging in a process of reframing meaning where useful. For instance, it makes a difference whether the staff member interprets the manager's response as acting out of a sense of (perhaps misguided) obligation to *make things work* to the best of his current understanding or whether his motivation is interpreted as *power hungry*. Of course, either or both could be valid, but it is important to imagine what interpretation(s) best empower one's own response (and the potential for others to respond in their turn) in ways that honour and develop the organizational and relational complexity. When faced with managerial behaviour, the staff member's rule for interpreting meaning will be inevitably partial, shaped by layers of context, and materialize in the form of the interpretation that the manager is *authoritarian*.

Choice of action (opportunity for reflexive response): our interpretation(s) of our own and another's meaning, motivation, and purpose will shape the decision we make to act; i.e., the next move in the conversation. We tend to invoke habitual *rules for action*, which are shaped by layers of contextual experience and current contexts of influence and manifested in what our senses and interpretations tell us.[5] The *rule for action* that could be invoked in this case might be *when faced with "authoritarian" behaviour I must retrieve power by complaining*. Moreover, the staff member's expressed description of the manager's *authoritarian* behaviour tacitly influences (by implicative force) the identity story about the manager that he is (say) *more interested in power than in hearing others' views*. This in turn shapes the emergent relational and cultural patterns. Thus, a mutually reinforcing pattern can be maintained, developed, or transformed, depending on the conscious choices made by the participants. In drawing attention to the reflexive opportunities in a communication, the aim is to encourage conscious purposeful communication.

Appreciative principle

- All action is meaningful
- Meaning and action are open to multiple interpretation and choice of response
- Evaluation and valuation are in contextual relationship
- Position self and other with care, robustness, vulnerability and empathy

All action is meaningful

In managing and facilitating critical consciousness an RI orientation will encourage us to appreciate that all action is meaningful and that our individual and collective histories and purposes give *logic* to our actions.[6] People act in ways that make sense to them and often these actions express attempts to belong and participate. Other people's ways of participating may not fit with our own or even with the defined purposes of an episode, but it makes a difference if we can acknowledge that they are meaningful.

Meaning and action are open to multiple interpretation and choice of response

RI also encourages an appreciation that our interpretations are partial, contextual, and unstable. This is a helpful position to take as it makes it more possible for us to take up a position of choice in relation to the kinds of realities we wish to create rather than be driven by established patterns that create rules unresponsive to the current context. Our actions could and should sometimes be discontinuous with what we feel and think. If we can inquire into, challenge, critique, and reframe habitual *rules* for making meaning and action, we may be more likely to create considered actions rather than habitual actions compelled by unreflective feeling or thought and not necessarily fitting with the systemic needs of a situation in all its complexity.

In the context of our example, the staff member might notice feelings of constraint and defence in his body and feelings of anger. He might find himself wanting to retaliate with a constraining response by complaining or might feel voiceless and capitulate. A reflexive orientation could help him to see that his habitual rules for meaning and action in this situation perpetuate an unwanted pattern. This appreciation might motivate him to challenge such rules and hypothesize about the contexts (particularly those of entitlement and obligation) that shape the interaction. In order to give a new pattern a chance he could attempt to act counter-intuitively (i.e., do something that doesn't *feel* right in the *natural* pattern but feels right in the context of a wider pattern that he is beginning to create). In this case, that could mean showing concern and interest for the manager's sense of obligation, moving more into a *we* position in attempting to understand the pressures on the manager and how he participates in that. Or it could mean finding a way to discuss the pattern itself and asking for the manager's help in disrupting it, thereby repositioning himself and the manager both subjectively and relationally. Alternatively, his reflexive appreciation might reinforce his position that protecting his own position is the most sensible action in the circumstances. He may consider that the appropriate action is to make his complaint more official. Even if the staff member continued the pattern with his manager, his participation would arguably be with more consciousness of its consequences.

Evaluation and valuation should be treated as in contextual relationship

A distinction is made here between AI and RI. In their crudest form, AI approaches can appear to try to eliminate all forms of *problem talk* from organizational life (Anderson et al., 2001; Barge & Oliver, 2003; Cooperrider, 1998).[7] AI represents a corrective to the kind of problem talk discussed earlier as first order critique. AI practitioners claim that if you talk about problems you create problems through the use of *deficit language* (Anderson et al., 2001). I want to argue that although one must take care with talk, a potentially pernicious consequence of the AI claim is that the evaluative baby is lost in the valuing bathwater. This can undermine trust. Asch (1952) has defined the conditions of trust as being: the ability to speak with sufficient openness; sufficiently shared perceptions of the present, and sufficiently shared hopes for the future. The injunction for organizational participants to treat each other affirmatively can, in these terms, stifle valid expressions of hurt, vulnerability, injustice, and ill-treatment, and potentially disallow discussion about implicit power relations. I propose that valuation and evaluation are best treated as if they are in a contextual relationship, not in an either/or relationship. Processes of evaluation should occur in the context of an appreciation and curiosity about the values and contributions of the individual in their context. At the same time, valuation should be communicated in the context of a reflexive critical consciousness. In RI, the question of how organizational and relational priorities are ordered and valued is open to observation and exploration, not assumed.

Position self and other with care, vulnerability and empathy

The AI injunction to treat self and other affirmatively, though useful for particular purposes in organizational dialogue, can potentially create superficial pseudo mutuality if treated slavishly. In RI the proposal is to create a relational context of shared humanity, sensitive to the vulnerability of both self and other and empathetic to the conditions of life that the other is invited or pressured into, not least, by oneself. The emphasis is more on the complexity of a person and their relationships of significance.

Complex principle

- The self referential, reflexive nature of humans.
- Structure and order are temporary punctuations in complex systems.
- Polarization is a common mechanism of simplification.
- The strange loop is a tool for managing the complexity of communication.

The self referential, reflexive nature of humans

Stacey, Griffin, and Shaw (2000) have argued that we need to think of organizations as complex responsive processes of relating and advocate drawing on the complexity sciences to do so. Their work has highlighted the radical unpredictability of the development of human processes. They point out that at one end of the spectrum a dominant voice in management theory is represented by language of prediction, regularity, and control. Causal links are connected to sophisticated tools for the prediction of behaviour. Systems are treated as objective realities that the manager can stand outside of and control. A counter position is that we are all members of complex networks that we cannot stand outside of *objectively*; self organizing processes are not subject to control and the task is to enhance the creative potential of participative processes. In a recent publication (2000), Stacey has proposed the notion of *bounded instability*, a place at the *edge of chaos* where learning and evolution can emerge. Both stability and chaos hold the potential for disintegration while bounded instability works hand in hand with reflexive consciousness and growth.

Structure and order are temporary punctuations in complex systems

In order to make life work in our organizations, we need, at times, to create structure and order out of chaos. However, complexity theory has helped us to understand that the simplifications of complexity that we make through structuring and ordering our realities need to be treated as temporary and imperfect and not as higher states (Eve, Horsfall, & Lee, 1997). Clarity and confusion need and give meaning to each other in the flow of organizational life (Cronen & Pearce, 1985). If a frame of learning can imbue our experiences of incoherence, recognized as temporary, and informing of structure and order, our experiences of coherence can be enriched (Senge, 1990).

Polarization is a common mechanism of simplification

Our mechanisms of simplification for managing complexity are varied, some more constructive than others. Polarization is a strategy that divides reality into dualistic opposites, for instance, good–bad, right–wrong, positive–negative. Although this strategy works in some situations, for instance where a decision is needing to be made about whether someone should be fired or not, in many situations the polarization strategy simplifies in a way that does an injustice to the richness and possibility inherent in communication. For instance, AI as a methodology stresses the importance of creating *positive spirit* and *positive energy* and asks us to inquire into what works well in the organization. I would suggest that such a position can create an unnecessary split between the positive and negative, relegating the so-called negative to the trash when there may be much of value in people's difficult experiences. What might matter is whether such difficulty is discussed in a context of reflexive inquiry.

The strange loop is a tool for managing the complexity of communication

When we use a polarizing defence we can sometimes experience an up and down pattern, at times "positive", at other times "negative". Such a pattern has been identified as a *strange loop* (Cronen, Johnson, & Lannamann, 1982; Oliver & Brittain, 2001; Oliver, Herosymowych, & Senko, 2003).[8] The strange loop is a special kind of hypothesis or narrative that takes the form of a paradoxical and polarized pattern. It is a useful hypothesis in those situations where we feel stuck or confused. The experience is one where we feel we are sliding from one position to its opposite with no stable vantage point, ending back where we started.

Cronen, Johnson, and Lannamann (1982) originally offered the strange loop form to explain paradoxes in communication. The loop structure works like a figure of eight rather than a circle. The levels of context described earlier, of culture, relationship, identity, and episode could, according to the original articulation of it, be polarized at each level. The significant development in the structuring of a strange loop offered by RI is that the story contexts above the polarized figure of eight pattern are defined as culture, relationship, and identity and the context of the pattern defined as episodic. That episodic pattern is further broken down into feeling, interpretation, and action levels. On the left-hand side there is a feeling of pressure (e.g., anxiety, anger) that is interpreted pessimistically and sets a context for a fragmented and closed reaction (e.g., blaming of others) that leads to a relief of pressure, then a more optimistic interpretation that facilitates a more open reaction, but this leads to pressure, and so on. This structuring of the pattern arguably renders the making of a loop more accessible by distinguishing between stories and patterns. Figure 3 shows the basic template of a strange loop. The content will be filled in with reference to the specific situation that needs explaining.

If we connect to our example and consider a loop from the staff member's perspective, we might hypothesize about the following (see Figures 4 and 5).

The participant in the pattern moves through a figure of eight over time. When moving down one side of the loop there is an experience of disconnection from the other side; i.e., a pattern of meaning is not formed, there is only a feeling of stuckness or confusion. The staff member experiences the pressure of a lack of participation when he is not consulted. The pressure mounts and he feels moved to speak up in a way that is interpreted as complaint. This provides some relief of pressure for him and means he

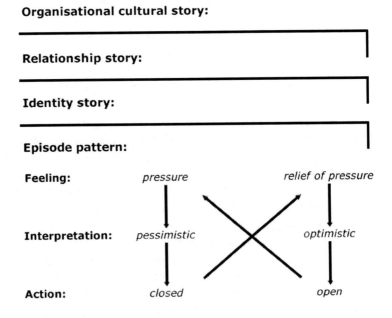

Organisational cultural story:

Relationship story:

Identity story:

Episode pattern:

Feeling:	pressure	relief of pressure
Interpretation:	pessimistic	optimistic
Action:	closed	open

Figure 3. The basic strange loop template

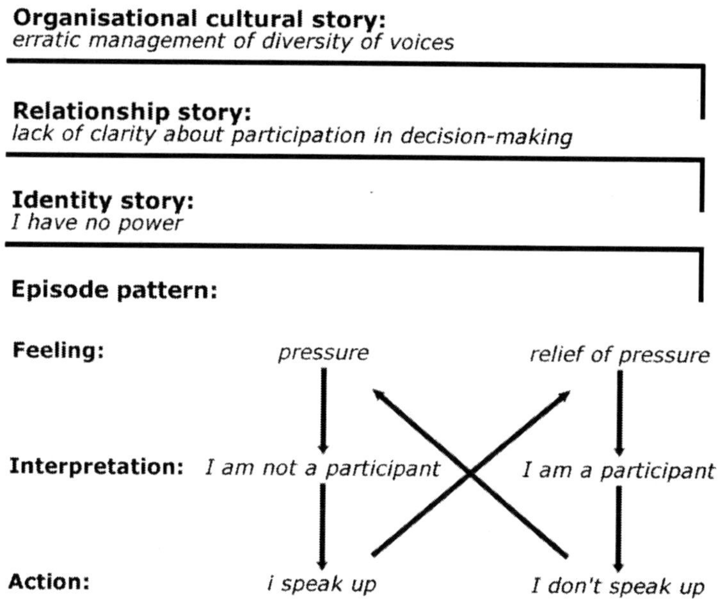

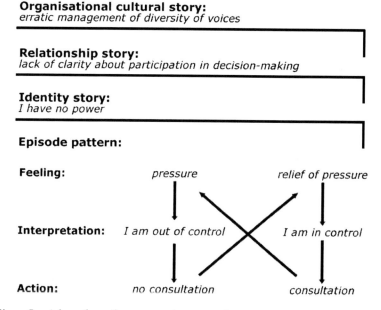

Organisational cultural story:
erratic management of diversity of voices

Relationship story:
lack of clarity about participation in decision-making

Identity story:
I have no power

Episode pattern:

Feeling: *pressure*   *relief of pressure*

Interpretation: *I am not a participant*   *I am a participant*

Action: *i speak up*   *I don't speak up*

Figure 4. A loop from the staff member's perspective

Organisational cultural story:
erratic management of diversity of voices

Relationship story:
lack of clarity about participation in decision-making

Identity story:
I have no power

Episode pattern:

Feeling: *pressure*   *relief of pressure*

Interpretation: *I am out of control*   *I am in control*

Action: *no consultation*   *consultation*

Figure 5. A loop from the manager's perspective

can experience himself as participating. He relaxes and chooses not to speak up but that then sets a context for the manager to feel anxious about the communication and he resists the staff member's input, acting in a controlling manner and so on.

The manager feels anxiety about the diversity of views in a consultation process and feels the need to take premature control, so engages in episodes of poor consultation but then gains some relief from the experience of control and can relax and engage in episodes of consultation that create anxiety and so on. Both behaviours create ripple effects for the other and invite their looped response.

The strange loop, as a special form of story-telling, enables clarity to be felt about unwanted patterns of experience but also facilitates speculation about how best to intervene. For instance, a consultant might identify an individual looped pattern for the staff member and/or for the manager, but can also help to build ideas with the team, or even wider contexts, about shared loop patterns. In this case, some ideas about intervention might be:

- in sharing the story of the pattern with other affected parties, people are enabled to reposition from blaming persons to focusing on a system of thinking and acting, potentially galvanizing a productive force for change;
- if one has been in a competitive pattern with another one can enlist their help in intervening in the pattern, thus restructuring the relationship;
- examination can be made of the contextual stories that hold the pattern in place and conscious choice engaged with to change such stories, e.g., to discuss together the system of decision-making;
- decisions can be made about when it is appropriate to consult and when to make autonomous decisions—for all parties;
- discussion can take place about alternative behaviours to complaint and control;
- at each stage of a loop there are choice points that can be identified and explored.

Summary

In this first chapter I have set out the frame of RI by offering a set of five principles drawn from the consultancy literature. Each principle offers a contribution to RI by emphasizing a particular dimension of reflexive practice. The systemic principle emphasizes the significance of pattern; the constructionist principle highlights the forming quality of communication; the critical principle acknowledges the political nature of communication and provides ways of facilitating humane evaluation; the appreciative principle encourages us to be open to a reality beyond our own egocentricity; the complex principle invites us to be open to the complexity of organizational life and to find strategies other than fragmentation and polarization in managing such complexity. Each principle overlaps and interweaves with the others to provide a theoretical and ethical frame for a set of RI practices. In turn, our RI practices potentially set a context for new developments in our RI frame.

Notes

1. I prefer the term "patterns lived and stories told" to "stories lived and stories told" (Pearce, 1994), as our experience is fragmented until a connecting narrative can be made, at which point it makes sense for it to be described as a story.
2. In foregrounding the moral place of the individual agent, the significance of the relational in shaping communication possibilities is not forgotten. The "I" and the "We" are in contextual relationship.
3. These levels can be treated as parallel to Bateson's levels of learning (1972).
4. Originally, Cronen and Pearce's "constitutive rule" (1985).
5. Originally, Cronen and Pearce's "regulative rule" (1985).
6. The Milan therapists developed the notions of positive, and then logical, connotation, which connoted the intentionality of people's actions as meaningful (Boscolo, Cecchin, Hoffman, & Penn, 1987). Another connected concept from Cronen and Pearce (1985) is that of "deontic logic", a reference to those patterns we live and stories we tell that carry moral meaning.
7. See Barge and Oliver (2003) for a wider discussion of appreciation in managerial practice.
8. Oliver, Herasymowych, and Senko have written a fieldbook about the strange loop as a tool in reflexive organizational practice and developed the pattern into six forms.

Reflexive inquiry tools for coordinating conversation

An RI orientation treats communication as the site of interest and as the place for change to happen. Thus, conversation is seen as holding power to make or break effective organizational action. For consultants in and with organizations, commissioned to facilitate development and change, the frames articulated in Chapter One facilitate sense-making in the work. They also stimulate the production of concrete tools for helping us to coordinate our thinking and action in conversation with others. RI draws on and develops *systemic, constructionist, critical, appreciative,* and *complexity* discourses to open up possibilities for new patterns. These tools are presented in this chapter, in the abstract, as forms of inquiry and reflection. There are many potential ways to develop inquiry and reflection and the precise details will need to be made with reference to the purposes and possibilities of specific situations. Part II shows how this might be done through use of RI tools with specific case studies.

Inquiry

The systemic tradition has made a unique contribution to inquiry methodologies through its writings on circular and reflexive questioning (Boscolo, Cecchin, Hoffman, & Penn, 1987; Penn, 1985; Tomm, 1985). The origins of the approach are in systemic therapy but the principles and patterns of questioning can be developed in an organizational context, both in a group setting and one to one. Inquiry is seen as synonymous with development, given that we are acting as if language creates our realities. The relevant question about practice becomes: *what kind of development am I making possible through my intervention*? The value of *public* inquiry in a group setting is that a group process is created through positioning participants both as speakers and listeners, enabling a complexity of learning to be experienced and observed. Different writers have offered a variety of categorizations for inquiry (Penn, 1985; Tomm, 1985). In Table 2, I offer a sample of the kinds of questions I find useful in generating reflexive action, referring back to the *patterns of connection* and *critical consciousness* models. These examples of questions represent a fraction of the potential for inquiry in a given situation. I use the hypothetical case example, imagining that a consultant is interviewing the staff member with manager as audience.

Table 2. Exploring macro communication (connecting contexts of self and other)

Context	Culture	Relationship	Identity
Self	"When you think about your way of communicating in the context of organizational culture, what sense does it make?"	"How do you see your rights and responsibilities to participate in decision making?"	"When did you first think of yourself as having trouble participating?" "What was happening at that time?"
Other	"How might the manager describe significant cultural stories in the organization that affect the ways you relate?"	"How might the manager describe the obligations to his staff that stem from his role?"	"How would you say the manager might describe himself as a manager?"

Table 3. Exploring micro communication (the interpretive act)

	Feeling	Interpretation	Action
Self	When you received x communication from the manager, what did you notice in your own body language? What feelings were you connected to? What feelings might you be disconnected from? Is your feeling one you have felt before in that relationship? When have you noticed a different feeling?	How do your feelings connect to your thoughts? What choice do you have in how you are interpreting the situation? Where does your sense of obligation come from? How did your stories about the relationship affect the way you interpreted it?	How did your interpretation shape your action? When you act in that way, how does it affect x? What would you like to create? If you created x, how might it affect your feeling and thinking? What might be an interaction that both would find productive?
Other	What did you notice about the manager's emotional response and body language? How might that have affected your response? How might the cultural pressures in the organization have shaped the manager's feelings? If he were more open about his feelings, how might you be affected?	If you thought of the manager as vulnerable and acting out of a sense of obligation, how would you make sense of what happened? How do you think he interpreted your response? What choices might you say the manager had in his response?	How did the manager respond to your response? Was that the response you hoped for? How might you have interpreted what happened differently if you felt you had more choice in creating the response that was best for the relationship (and the organization)?

The change cycle

The notion of a change cycle is to be found in many writings about change (Cooperrider, 1998, Kolb, 1984). AI methodology, for instance, offers us a generative cycle in the form of discovery, dream, design, and delivery (see Figure 6). The discovery phase classically explores what has worked well in relation to the theme at hand, e.g., the *development of team communication*. Small groups begin to explore experience and their feedback is facilitated in the larger group. The dream phase enables an imagining of the best of what could be for a particular organization, community, or team, relating values and principles to core practices. The design phase typically becomes more concrete and encourages the making of proposals and decisions. The delivery phase ensures that decisions will be followed through and organizes how that will be achieved. This form of dialogue allows for a process of divergence and convergence, delaying the convergence favoured by *problem solving models* until a rich and creative layering of discussion and negotiation occurs about an ideal future in the dreaming phase (Hammond,

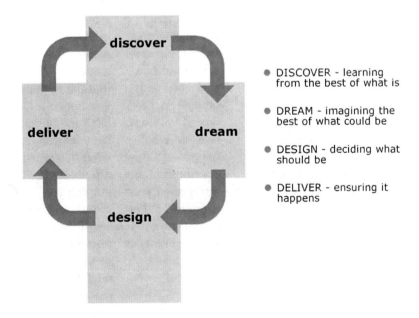

Figure 6.   4D cycle

1998). The AI process disallows a focus on fragility, emphasizing the importance of learning from success. While I have found this form of a change cycle productive, in my work I have learnt that a focus on fragility can be generative in the context of reflexive agreements and commitments. Also, I have learnt that the frame of RI can generate many forms, the specifics of each design needing to be worked out in the context of the needs of a particular consultancy situation (see Chapter Four for further detail).

The *cross* symbol represented here was developed in the context of work with religious organizations. I decided to preserve the symbolism to convey the notion of crossroads or crisis, etymologically connected to the meaning of turning point.

Reflection

Public reflection has been proposed as a basis for learning and, in particular, its potential valued for developing a *community of inquiry*. "Reflection is the practice of . . . stepping back to ponder the meaning to self and others in one's immediate environment about what has recently transpired" (Raelin, 2001, p. 11). Raelin advocates the facilitation of three levels of reflection—content, process, and premise, in situations where understanding of an organizational experience needs to be developed. This proposal has value in the way it focuses and links different levels of meaning and learning, though there are many forms public reflection could take, some of which are explored below.

Elkjaer (2001, p. 440), writing about the learning organization, describes how John Dewey, the American pragmatist, connected reflection processes with situated learning processes. Reflection, he argues, works creatively when it allows for inquiry into *situations of uncertainty*. He suggests that meaning is created when connections are made between experience and its consequences. Learning develops when those meanings are linked to present concerns.

I would propose that a public reflection process facilitates meta-communicative learning. Its benefits can be multi-levelled but in any given circumstance would have a specified focus and aim. The learning potential developed may be at cultural, relational, and individual levels. At a cultural level, regular reflection practices can help to build a community of practice, challenging and enhancing cultural patterns and stories (Lave & Wenger, 1991). At a relational level, learning can occur about patterns of communication and effective processes developed. At an individual level, meaning can be opened up so that interpretive acts can be connected to social processes and stories enriched through building patterns of connection.

One important source for inspiring reflection is the systemic therapy tradition where particular rules have been developed to facilitate the opening up of meaning and the preservation and enhancement of the dignity of participants in a therapeutic session. A reflection in this context takes the form of a conversation about a conversation. The therapist and her team speak about the conversation the therapist has been having with the client, in front of the client (Andersen, 1987). The conversation between therapist and client then resumes, linking back to the reflection. In an organizational consultancy context, I am suggesting a public reflection could be used in a similar way, as a means to enhance dialogue, learning, relationship, and organizational culture through the same means of a conversation about a conversation. The guidelines developed in the systemic therapy context are expanded below to fit an organizational context. They are linked to the organizational example that has been developed so far.

Guidelines for reflecting conversations

- Decide the focus for reflection e.g. the obligations and entitlements imagined for manager and staff member;
- decide how to position participants as speakers and listeners e.g. manager and staff member could be audience to their team's reflection;
- position speakers in the reflection with a clear purpose, e.g., to reflect on cultural and team patterns that shape the pattern of relationship in order to help to make sense of the pattern;
- position listeners to the reflection with a clear purpose, for example, to look for openings in the dialogue for repositioning;
- give those who have been spoken about in the third person position the last word on what was and was not meaningful for them;

- create a second layer of reflection on the learning in the process, positioning all participants in the same learning position;
- enable participants to speak from their positions in the func-tional hierarchy while encouraging the participation of all voices;
- use the guidelines for reflexive inquiry described above.

The domains model

Inquiry and reflection offer extensive possibilities for developing meaning and action. However, the consultant using RI needs to be able to access a range of subject positions and relationship patterns to maximize leverage for intervention. It helps to have access to a frame that allows for multi-positioning, and provides a mechanism for reflexive, situated decision-making. The *domains model* has been proposed as a useful frame for hypothesizing and guiding action (Maturana & Varela, 1987; Lang, Little, & Cronen, 1990). Its usage has since been extended, both as a frame for hypothesizing and as a tool for structuring conversation (Oliver & Brittain, 2001).

The *domains model* provides another way of working with context, meaning, and action. It was originally developed to help professionals acting in complex contexts (e.g., social workers engaging in child protection work) to separate out contexts so that they could decide which definition of relationship, with its associ-ated rights and responsibilities, and which kind of conversation they should be emphasizing at any given point in time, enabling them to foreground and name, where appropriate, the facilitative and evaluative functions of their work.

In a similar way it can be a helpful tool where there is confusion within an organizational process about the conversational context. For instance, is a manager making a demand or a suggestion when asking someone to do something in a particular way? The model invites us to ask ourselves which context (domain) is strongest in influence, or requires most attention, in a given situation.

In the model we are invited to treat the (organizational) world as if it is separated out into three *meta contexts* or *domains*: of *produc-tion, explanation,* and *aesthetics.* Within each domain the individual actor values a particular way of seeing and acting in that world. His task is to decide which domain to temporarily emphasize, while appreciating that the other domains are still operative but informed and contextualized by the requirements of the domain needing emphasis. The model helps us to challenge a pattern whereby we might act in one domain as if that is THE way of seeing and acting in the world, rather than ONE position taken for particular purposes, in the knowledge that the position is temporary and partial and operating within a wider domains context.

For instance, in a training course on performance management, some managers talked as if they had one style of management when they referred to their *management style*. The course proposed that in the context of performance management, the domains model could help managers decide, with reference to the needs of the situation, whether their (relationship and communication) style should be more in the evaluative domain (of production), where they would be emphasizing assessment of performance, or in the more facilitative domain (of explanation), where they would be more likely to be negotiating a form of coaching activity with their staff.

I show the distinctions and relationships between the domains by using the notion of moral order, framing contextual levels within

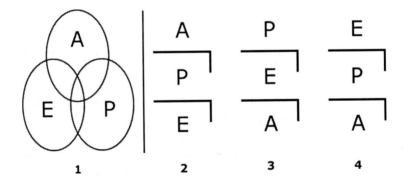

1   The model can be pictured as if each domain overlaps the others, and with the domain of aesthetics in hierarchical relationship to the domains of production and explanation

2-4.1 Alternatively the domains can be represented as being in contextual relationship with each other in a variety of ways (three examples are shown). Depending on one's situation one can decide where in the levels of context to position each domain

Figure 7.   The domains model: aesthetics, production and explanation

an overt moral structure that maps the domains of production and explanation on to modernist and postmodern discourses and frames the domain of aesthetics as a space for reflexive reflection and decision making (see Table 4).

Use of the domains model to structure conversation

My commitment to making practical theory encouraged the extension of the model from a tool for hypothesizing into a tool for creating boundaries and rules for conversation as well (Oliver & Brittain, 2001). I have used the model to manage processes of inquiry and reflection, with the aim of enabling a reflexive multi-positioning within these processes and facilitating a detachment from fixed ideas and practices.[1]

The model can be used in a variety of ways. The basic form is that three consecutive conversations occur, corresponding to the three domains (Figure 8). The rules for the talk within each domain are identified and it is the task of the consultant to ensure that those rules are kept. The same group of people can have three consecutive conversations or three different groups could have three different conversations with the others as audience.

For instance, during a process of needs assessment for management training it was clear that a management group was at such odds in its vision of management that the members talked at cross purposes. Some people talked of management from a modernist perspective as if it involved processes of planning, organization, evaluation, and measurement; others treated it as a more postmodern phenomenon, using the language of facilitation and consultation. There seemed to be a lack of awareness that people were speaking out of different contexts, although there was frustration shown. In being invited to discuss their management training needs from the perspective of the three domains in turn, each individual was able to inhabit both discourses and treat both as valid but incomplete on their own. The consultants invoked the notion of temporary positioning, allowing the group to speak with a shared purpose.

In the domain of explanation they were encouraged to speculate about the purpose of developing management training, linking different contributions, imagining potential futures, showing

Table 4. Moral order in the domains of production, explanation and aesthetics

Domain	Production	Explanation	Aesthetics
Cultural discourse	Modernist; valuing of order, control, structure, hierarchy, reduction of complexity, dichotomies, clarity	Postmodern; valuing of complexity, curiosity, divergence, partiality, narrative, multiple perspectives	RI principles; commitment to critical consciousness
Definition of relationship	Concern with power; individual coherence is emphasized at the expense of coordination of meaning with others. *I am your boss and require you to act in x way.*	Concern for coordinating rights and responsibilities with others; relational connection and coherence emphasized. *What effect might it have if I suggested x?*	Concern for accountability and responsibility for the relational contexts created in communication. *What are we learning from this management process?*
Person and subject position	Commitment to first person position; opinion, demand and advice giving encouraged. *I think . . . I expect . . . I require . . .*	Commitment to second person position; inquiry, facilitation and reflection encouraged. *What are your ideas about . . .?*	Commitment to reflexive contextual decision-making about the positioning of self and others. *What did we make?*
Obligation	To achieve clarity with a view to making the right decision *I should decide . . .*	make meaning; explore and reflect on connections. *How does x link with y?*	Link meaning to decision-making; co-ordination of domain, role and task. *Having explored, how should we act?*

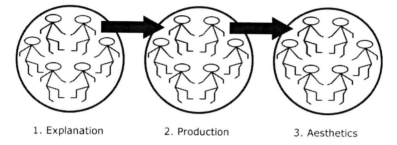

1. Explanation   2. Production   3. Aesthetics

Figure 8.   Consecutive group conversations in domains

curiosity about each other's ideas, enquiring into people's assumptions. In the domain of production they were encouraged to state strong opinions, even to argue, to discuss "the truth" about what should be done, to think in terms of right and wrong. In the domain of aesthetics they were encouraged to think about how any of these ideas could be coherent with the organization's mission and purpose, how the ideas produced from each phase of the discussion could be integrated to create a sufficiently complex and coherent way forward.

Another possibility is to create an inquiry/interviewing process in the domain of aesthetics and employ two reflecting discussions, which represent the other two domains (Figure 9). The decision about in which order to take the discussions is a matter of judgment in relation to the purposes and dynamics of the situation. The guidance above about the management of reflexivity still applies. This can be helpful in separating the making of meaning from the making of decisions. In my experience, many meetings or problem-solving processes flounder either because these two contexts and purposes are not sufficiently separated, and then integrated, or because there is too much enthusiasm to move into the domain of production and fix the problem before it is sufficiently understood.

Rules for the domain of production

Participants are encouraged to speak within a discourse of dichotomy and convergence; a search for clarity is encouraged. Preoccupations with structure, contract, and concern for decision-making and

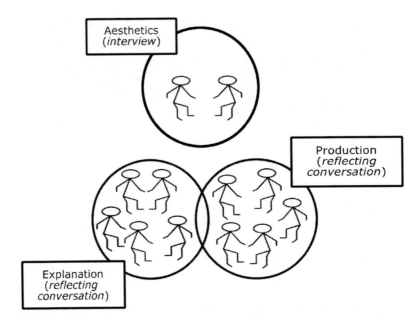

Figure 9.   Interview and reflecting conversations in domains

action are likely to be expressed. Legitimate behaviours are opinion-giving, advice-giving, planning, argument, and persuasion.

Rules for the domain of explanation

Participants are encouraged to speak within a discourse of complexity, curiosity, and connection. Attempts will be made to make sense and develop stories and narratives of connection. Curiosity will be expressed about the views of others and inquiry made with a view to identify and develop organizational patterns. Legitimate behaviours are questioning, connecting elements of stories, facilitation of the views of others.

Rules for the domain of aesthetics

Participants are encouraged to speak within an RI discourse with a view to linking the learning from the domains of explanation and production. A concern for coherence and fit will be expressed, with the aims of facilitating meaning, purpose, and effective action.

Legitimate behaviours would be reflexive observation of patterns of connection and disconnection between the two domains and attention given to the connections and coherence with the wider organizational task and the purposes of the consultation.

An example of use in the context of our running example could be that the team could participate in three consecutive discussions, facilitated by the consultant, on the theme of *participation in decision-making*. The manager may be placed as audience or as participant. If they begin in the domain of explanation they could inquire into their different experiences and narratives about participation, draw out their stories, exploring the contextual logic for the patterns they find. In the domain of production they could discuss how they felt such patterns ought to be, sharing opinions and arguing for particular proposals. In the domain of aesthetics they could take a systemic view of the two previous discussions and reflect on the fit that is needed with team, role, task, and organizational purposes.

Summary

Chapter Two has offered an incomplete and emerging set of practices for coordinating conversation in inquiry processes in ways that are coherent with the frame set out in Chapter One. These practices have included inquiry into macro and micro communication contexts, change cycles, reflection processes, and the domains model.

As an organizational consultant interested in the power of conversation to make change, a key concern for me has been how to enable participants to discuss concerns, difficulties, dilemmas, injustices, hurts, and fragilities. Whereas AI addresses this dilemma by focusing on the learning from what works well and the hopes for a better future, RI attempts to treat these subjects as meaningful and significant sites for learning in themselves. The tools used for such reflexive evaluation should become more accessible to the reader when they are understood in the context of the detailed case studies offered in Part II.

Note

1.   This way of working with the domains model has been developed with colleague Graham Brittain.

PART II

WORKING WITH
REFLEXIVE INQUIRY

CHAPTER THREE

The monks' tale: a community learning to co-exist

C hapter Three articulates the development of RI interventions over time, in a context of hurt and conflict in a community. It highlights in detail three structured exercises, variations of the tools identified in Chapter Two, from consultancy work with a male religious order. It will attempt to show how these structures express an RI orientation through connection back to the RI principles laid out in Chapter One.

Over the past few years a colleague[1] and I have been working with a male religious community. I was invited to work with them when they heard about my work with AI. The community presented their concerns in a language of conflict, demoralization, and breakdown in communication. Most members of the community experienced severe distress; loss of membership became a potential threat. At the beginning of the work people talked in the following terms:

It's hard to experience hope.

There is envy and competition but we don't talk about it.

There is a lack of charity in our talk about others.

We don't recognize each other.

We need to drop our masks.

We are shrinking daily.

We need to face the truth about ourselves as a community.

I ask myself "Has my life had meaning?"

The breakdown had been triggered by a crisis two years previously, when a personnel decision had been made that caused a split in the community. They defined themselves as being in *two camps.* The leader, with a group of supporters, was on one side, and a group who challenged the leadership on the other side. This experience of split was distressingly challenging to a perceived obligation of wholeness that was felt should characterize community. However, whenever attempts had been made to resolve the conflict, the split pattern seemed to become more entrenched.

When we began work with the community, the decision was made initially to use an AI process to attempt to create a discontinuity from existing patterns, encouraging a shared empathic relational experience, which could work as an enabling context for future work. Members of the group were asked to explore the meaning of membership of the community through articulating their stories of belonging and connectedness. We asked, *how come you chose to belong to this community? What were your stories about the community at the time of joining? What were your hopes for yourself and the community when you joined?* Using these stories as a base, we helped people to begin to create images of the future—of the community and of the individual and his connection to community. The AI process had a successful impact in that it did enable a new, inquiring relational context to emerge, not substituting for but juxtaposed with the dislocated experience that had developed. People began to say, *well, we can still talk to each other; these are stories we have never told each other and it is good to hear them.* However, what was also said was, *the conflict has not been touched and it still touches us under the surface.* It was apparent to the consultants that the group experienced a struggle to create images of the future. Images were fragmented and associated with fear and a preoccupation with death.

Within the consultancy work a paradoxical pattern or *strange loop* constraining meaningful communication was observed. We noticed that when a concern or difficult feeling was "needing" to be named, a fear of encounter was created with the consequence of invoking a kind of pseudo safety. Thus, the experience would not get named, with the consequence of withdrawal from engagement. However, the context of disengagement would build such a feeling of discomfort, given the discourses of brotherhood in the community, that the need for challenge or critique would be invoked; thus, there would be a naming and its concomitant fear of destructive consequences in encounter. And so this looped communication would endure. From the interviewing, observation, and experience of the *patterns lived,* the consultants hypothesized the following stories to be constraining communication and setting a context for the looped pattern depicted in Figure 10.

We, the consultants, were faced with deeply entrenched discourses and patterns of interaction that made sense in the contexts shown above. The community shared a long history of discomfort with difference and with engagement (for example, they

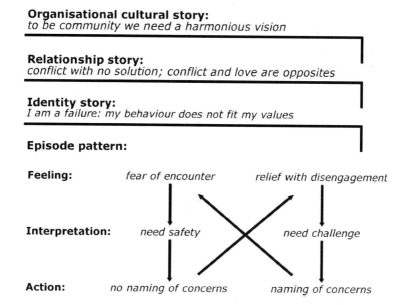

Figure 10.   Loop of pseudo safety

had always experienced a difficulty about sharing meaning in relation to their religious and spiritual life for fear that too much difference would be revealed). The conflict about the justice of leadership
action had seemed to deepen fears about irreconcilable differences.
We noticed in the larger group a stifling tentativeness, which, we
hypothesized, inferred a great fear about opening the subject up
again, while at the same time a sense of despair that if it wasn't
addressed the future of the community was endangered. Two individuals came to us privately, speaking in a very different way from
the tentativeness shown in the wider group. They expressed
despair about change yet dread that if there were no change they
would feel obliged to leave the community.

We felt, after these conversations, that we ourselves were in a
loop—that if we addressed the conflict head on we would create a
defensive reaction, yet, if we didn't address it explicitly, we would
be avoiding something important at the heart of the community and
not doing our job. We felt we needed to try to understand this
conflict at the heart, treat it as precious and protect it, not through
polarization but in a way that made the community less fragile.
We took the decision to interview all members of the community
privately and formally. We explained how we experienced the
dilemma described above and shared the loop with them. We
suggested that we would be compounding the community's
dilemma if we enacted the pattern in the same way as the community. From the interviews we would be seeking understanding about
key themes and concerns in relation to this dilemma and saw our
responsibility as feeding these themes back, having listened to the
heart and mind of the community even if they were normally themes
they felt they should protect. The community agreed, with relief that
the consultants were concerned for the fragile, but with hope that
they were helping them (potentially) to move out of their stuckness.

This intervention had the function of enabling us, the consultants, to move outside the loop that we were in, by finding a way
of speaking of a pattern instead of enacting it, thus providing one
model for the community as to how to extricate from the loop. It
enabled us to articulate *unspeakable* dilemmas and paradoxical
patterns that were holding the community in their thrall, from a
position of legitimacy, thus setting a context for an intervention to
move things on.

Reflexive inquiry intervention

Following the interviews, we shared our "insights". We said how touched we were at the thought that had gone into preparation for the interviews. Concern and care for the community was palpable.

Consistent with our previous message, we shared the feeling that we needed to help the community speak the unspeakable. We proposed that the unspeakable related to fears about death of community. However, the polarized behaviour was making that more likely to happen. The community did not feel it was in a sufficiently healthy place to welcome new members and even if others stayed in the community (and some were threatening not to), the feeling of fragmentation felt like a kind of death.

We said that in our listening we had heard about the destructive effects of the split and had heard the desire for change, but appreciated that people needed to learn how to change. We suggested the community needed to practise new ways of relating and we had designed an exercise for that purpose.

An inquiry process was proposed that aimed to facilitate self and group reflexivity, positioning each participant's behaviour as contributing to the systemic pattern of connections. All twenty-four participants were asked to work with another with whom they felt they could work. All participants stayed working in the one room.

Stage 1

Write a statement (paragraph or less) about how you feel you have contributed to misunderstanding, mistrust and distancing in community life, particularly in relation to the conflict that has triggered so much unhappiness.

(Here we gave examples of how people may have contributed—through blaming others without seeking understanding, through silence, through withdrawal.)

Stage 2

Working with another, read the other's statement—interview each other from a position of curiosity and concern about the assumptions in the statement.

Stage 3

Write a response in the form of a letter to the other saying:

- what effect it has had on you to experience this conversation;
- what you have understood about the other's motivations and concerns;
- what you wish for the other now.

Stage 4

Share letters and make verbal responses.

Stage 5

Reflect in the large group about the experience and how it has affected your stories about identity, relationship and community.

Group reflection

Verbal responses to the exercise included:

> The exercise fitted with our own valuing of confession and helped things to begin to come out into the light. What were stumbling blocks could become building blocks.

> It is the first time I have been challenged to take responsibility for my contribution to the malaise. Previously I have tried to analyse what went wrong or try to put it right—this is a new position to be in.

> It is a new experience to spend time with one another.

> Focusing on ones own vulnerability makes one more attractive to the other and paradoxically helps to build strength

Revisiting RI principles

I will place the tools and practices described above in the context of RI principles.

Systemic principle

The members of the community were in agreement that they participated in unwanted patterns, but were unclear about how their patterns of relating created the demoralizing consequences that they experienced. This reflexive inquiry into the workings of the community, set in a context of shared fragility and responsibility, an important *psychological contract*, facilitated a developing consciousness about such connections. As such, it represented a turning point in its relationship to itself. In this, a shared moral awareness was created about responsibility for constructing the future. Use of the word *story* facilitated an appreciation that each position could be less entrenched, inviting people into a position where they might see how a new story could be developed. One important way in which the context was widened was to make the individual story, a relational and community story. The exercise was intended to challenge a pattern of "side taking" and facilitate more of an image of a web of connections—of individual contributions that were shaped by and shaped the whole.

Constructionist principle

Within the exercise, all participants were positioned with the same task of reflecting together, in a relational context, on the connections between their own behaviour and the patterns of community. The inference was that all had played their part in contributing to the whole and that the communications made in this exercise held new potential for shaping community and relational culture. In sharing the loop hypothesis, the consultants were encouraging members of the community to reflect on the role of polarization in the making of their communication and encouraging new relational behaviour in the exercise, hoping that it would have an implicative reflexive effect on identity, relationship, and culture.

This *confessional* exercise provided a new vocabulary for accountability. The *lived pattern* only legitimized a calling to account of each other in the context of a right/wrong polarity, accountability being conducted through the mechanism of creating *third persons*; for example, *we have poor leadership*. In that context, mistrust of the motivation of others was rife. The new form of accountability invited speaking and listening by *first persons* to *second persons*, in the context of an invited sensitization to the impact of contributions on the other through the ways the exercise was worded, for example, *what do you wish for the other?*—the embedded message being that one has the other's interests at heart. Through the invitation to inquire into the assumptions of the statement each person made, the *moral logic*, i.e., the *stories of obligation* and *entitlement* within participants' actions, were opened up for examination. The loop gives some clues as to what these might be and how they might need to change for movement to take place. For instance, in the context of a relational story of conflict, the obligation becomes, *for the sake of justice, I must win*, whereas a more constructive story of obligation might be, *for the sake of justice, I should risk sharing more of my own motivations and needs*.

Critical principle

The enactment of *stories of obligation* invites and constrains particular experiences of self—in this case, a self that struggles with feelings of anger and rejection towards others and a feeling of demoralization about not being able to change such a position. The exercise was designed to facilitate consciousness of the choices involved in these pulls and pushes. Inquiry into the assumptions in each person's statement allowed the potential for respectful challenge. The enactment of curiosity represents, in itself, a structural change. It encourages humility towards one's own position while, at the same time, encouraging a sharing of responsibility for the development of the other person's story. In the group reflection, one person expressed how they were made more *attractive* to each other through the exercise.

In asking people to consider how they had contributed to the difficulties, we were drawing attention to how people used or silenced their voices. It was repeatedly stated that a characteristic pattern (part of the loop) was shown in the way that people were fearful of asking questions about how others felt or what they thought. This way of positioning self in relation to others was, through the exercise, seen as having an active and destructive effect.

We were also drawing attention to the mechanisms of critique in the group. First order critique was the characteristic *us and them* pattern. People were blamed either for supporting an unjust process or for disloyalty to the leadership. No other position had seemed possible. It seemed impossible for motivation to be ascribed as complex and that people were *acting for the good of the community*. As was stated many times, *we caricature each other*. The exercise invited second order critique through positioning individuals as reflecting on their own contribution to a pattern and facilitating a connection between development for the individual and the ways another might be able to encourage such development. It also facilitated third order critique in the way it invited the community to take a reflexive position to how community was created through individual behaviours and relational patterns.

Appreciative principle

The exercise was designed to convey that people's actions were meaningful even if not desirable. It was also an attempt to convey the usefulness of seeking understanding and opening up stories of motivation. In this, people experienced the witnessing of the commitments, struggles, and intentions of the other. The lived pattern was reframed from a *story of failure* to one of shared humility, vulnerability, compassion, and generosity about the intentions and limitations of self and other.

In opening up inquiry about the *confessional* statement, the message was communicated that there are no fixed meanings. In inviting people to consider and share what they wished for the other, obligations were subtly constructed in relation to the other for one's own development (and that of the community) and concrete help provided about ways to go forward. The breaking of habitual patterns was made more possible in the context of that shared good will and the development of a shared vocabulary for reflexivity. People talked of the possibility of being able to say, *we are in that pattern again—help me get out of it*. Arguably, conditions for trust were being laid down in this cautious attempt to be open about one's own position and open towards the other.

Complexity principle

The strategy that members of the community used for managing experiences of discomfort was one of enacting a feeling (of fear) rather than speaking about it and exploring its meaning. This fragmentation precipitated a strange loop pattern of oscillating encounter and withdrawal. The fear that was associated with encounter was thus temporarily but not permanently disposed of. The consultants hypothesized a difficulty in seeing and holding the complexity of the pattern of connection. The difficulty was connected to a problematic shared belief that community meant harmony. In the group reflection, the consultants offered the framing of co-unity as a model for community rather then harmony. The fear of a lack of shared vision had meant that discussion at the level of vision and strategy never took place in any grounded way. Behaviours that seemed to indicate extreme differences became feared as representative of division and incommensurability; fears bred more fears.

Participants described how the exercise facilitated an experience of respect and empathy for the other's difference. When the other described his experience, its difference was allowed to co-exist rather than being heard as undermining or blaming. Someone described how *I felt respect for him for being able to tell me this*. Reflecting on the positive/negative split I perceive as embedded in AI, I would suggest that great care needs to be given to what counts as positive or negative for a group and for the individuals in that group. I would want to point out that in this case, in the context of the *grammar*[2] of this particular religious community, what counted as *positive* was the ability to own one's part in a difficulty rather than blaming the other side or trying to fix what went wrong. Participants were able to link the *grammar* of the exercise with the *grammar* of *confession*. What was "affirmed" in this case was the growing relational ability of individuals to create richer patterns of life and the motivation to want to do this, rather than the behaviour of individuals *per se* (Boscolo, Cecchin, Hoffman, & Penn, 1987).

The representation of the community's experience in the form of a strange loop enabled the focus to become more complex— rather than two opposing sides the focus became a *system of rules for meaning-making and action*, which showed itself in *patterns lived and stories told*. This systemic focus helped to detoxify the poisonous *us and them* discourse that had been governing relationships. It also created a feeling of all being *in the same boat*, which restructured the polarized *us and them* discourse into a *we are all suffering fallible humans* discourse. I hope it created the increased potential for the giving and receiving of help. The seeds were sown for that possibility.

The loop also identified particular stories that were thought to be problematic, allowing for grounded practical developments in community life. In a later intervention, the consultants invited the community to address the question of vision and strategy by facilitating the creation of a group that was to investigate the relationship between the community and its theological college. The group members developed terms of reference and were to account for their work to the community during the consultation processes.

In an attempt to consider alternative options to encounter and withdrawal, the core form of engagement (a weekly meeting) was discussed (among others) and was redesigned to allow for more openness and less competitiveness. A turn-taking strategy was created for leading a discussion and part of the meeting was given over to sharing the experience of the week in a meaningful way rather than the previous *rote* contributions.

Continuing the monks' tale

The RI chronicled above supported the desire for change and provided new possibilities for vocabularies of meaning and action. However, the intervention created its own fragilities in that it facilitated more of a state of *not knowing*. This was helpful in the context of increasing the repertoire of responses in the community necessary for change to occur, but it also sowed the seeds for further loops when *not knowing* might trigger anxiety. It was important to construct and reinforce a frame of learning for the consultation process and, we hypothesized, the transformation of anxiety into openness to learning could only come in time, needing practice for it to feel grounded as a response. We came to realize that a position of curiosity towards the patterns of which one is a part is not a response that can be conjured up on demand. People need to want to be curious, to learn that it has more beneficial effects than withdrawal and need to learn how to do it. We developed the appreciation that we needed to help the community to practise the ability to show curiosity and to reflect on what is heard and noticed. Many members of the community had lived together for forty years and had developed their patterns over that time. This is an unusual group—neither family nor organization but with dimensions of both.

For the first two years of our work with the community we visited them four times a year for three days each time. In that time, the ability to live reflexively with communication and to learn from these reflections did develop at different levels and in different ways. Positions were changed, people's stories about each other became more rounded; people talked openly of their patterns and showed the ability to engage in second order critique; the language of conflict was less apparent. However, on the consultants' return it would sometimes be said, *after you have gone our new abilities seem a lot less robust.* We took care to create the conditions for the group to learn from its own experience and for our work with it to have specified purposes designed by and with the group. We were very keen not to create a situation of inappropriate dependence, while at the same time we felt the group was not quite ready to launch off alone. However, we came to see that a huge stumbling block was presented by a forthcoming leadership election.

We perceived an atmosphere of demoralization in the group. The belief was expressed that no one was electable as leader (given that the election system required a two-thirds majority). The current leader was intending to be available for re-election and although it seemed that two or three others were also "available" for consideration, the common practice of the community was for there not to be an explicit discussion until there was a vote and, certainly, canvassing was frowned on. Demoralization seemed to go hand in hand with paralysis. One person wrote to us saying that the future was hopeless unless the current leader stepped down. We wrote back in a way that encouraged the person to act on his concerns while challenging the idea that the future was so contingent on the leadership. Consistent with our previous communications we invited a consideration of the conditions for effective *followership* (which were needed in his actions now). Although we had facilitated some small group work to encourage individuals, for the sake of the whole, to consider their own position and actions in relation to the election, with a view to the community taking responsibility for itself, the feeling of discomfort was difficult for them to experience and it looked as if this structure (and the learning up until then) might not be enough. But then something happened that was supportive of the idea from complexity theory that where there is the most noise there is the push for change (Oliver, Herasymowych, & Senko, 2003). One individual, a supporter of the current leader, behaved in an uncharacteristic way by opening up the discussion, setting a context of obligation to the community (rather than loyalty to his "candidate"), saying *we must talk about this. We must be clearer what each other think. We have our future in our hands.* The current leader was asked (and agreed) to leave the room and the group was able to have a candid discussion about the possibilities, which did not get stuck in supporter "camps" but created a grounding for an effective voting process. The outcome was a successful vote. In other words, the process worked for the community; a new leader was selected who had the majority of support from the community.

The consultants arrived to facilitate a reflection about the process. We faced and witnessed a range of feelings—relief, excitement, concern, euphoria, sadness, loss. The overwhelming sense, though, was that the community itself had shown its ability to change through this process and that feeling seemed to create a lightness in the group.

We met with a small group that had been charged with commissioning the next stage of the work. An interesting pattern of communication was shown:

One person expressed euphoria, saying how pleased he and others were at the change in the community following the election. On hearing this, another expressed pessimism, saying he was concerned that there was too much euphoria around, that it wasn't grounded and that he feared nothing had really changed, just a different person in power. The first person interpreted this communication as a diminishment, saying, *I feel stupid and naïve.* The second person said, *I fear that critique will get lost.* Both were upset by this exchange, feeling that their own position could not be heard and accepted. We discussed with this small group how it seemed difficult for the group to allow optimism and pessimism to co-exist and proposed that this was an interesting challenge to take to the large group. We hypothesized that the strange loop below was representative of the pattern experienced, as shown in Figure 11.

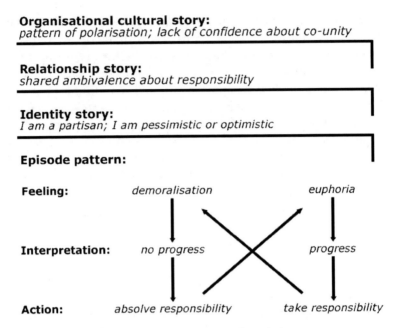

Organisational cultural story:
pattern of polarisation; lack of confidence about co-unity

Relationship story:
shared ambivalence about responsibility

Identity story:
I am a partisan; I am pessimistic or optimistic

Episode pattern:

Figure 11. Either/or approach to optimism and pessimism

The narrative for this loop goes something like this.

In the context of the draw of an old pattern of polarization and insufficiently practised new pattern to engender confidence, a relational story of ambivalence gets enacted. To take responsibility for self and the group requires facing difficult themes and dilemmas such as the future of the community and the future for oneself in the community. This can be felt as a profound challenge. The temptation is to avoid consciousness and not to hold and face the complexity of what is involved but to adopt a right/wrong position of optimism or pessimism. The community in this context will enact episodes that have an either/or unstable quality. These episodes will follow a pattern of an experience of demoralization or pessimism, which will lead to the idea that there is no progress. At this point the responsibility of someone outside the self is invoked such as the leader. However, if the leader is responsible, the individual can become euphoric or, in less extreme terms, optimistic, and a feeling of progress can be achieved. In that context, it becomes possible for a shared responsibility to develop. However, when the realities of responsibility are faced, pessimism or demoralization comes into play. And so the cycle goes on unless someone behaves differently (as someone did prior to the election) or the stories holding the pattern in place are challenged.

Reflexive inquiry intervention

We shared our experience of the small group in the large group and named it as a problem of polarization and fragmentation. We suggested that a new ability would be shown if the community could treat apprehension and hope as in a relationship of co-existence, not either/or, and that these qualities not be embodied in persons but the community hold responsibility for both. An exercise was offered for developing these abilities:

Stage 1

In pairs, interview each other about what developments you have noticed in self, relationship and community in the period just before and after the election? Describe these observations in the detail of events and situations that have arisen.

Then explore the struggles you have noticed.

What attitudes and behaviours made development possible even though struggle was part of the experience?

Stage 2

Reflect on your learning in the pair.

Stage 3

Building on your learning, write down and share:

What would you wish the other to change in attitude and behaviour?

What will you do to encourage and support these developments?

Stage 4

Community reflection and critique.

Revisiting RI principles

Systemic principle

The group were positioned in the exercise to observe the relationship between development and struggle, to see how they were in a pattern that connected. In inviting participants to inquire into the attitudes and behaviours that made development possible, they were invited into a learning position about their own contribution to the whole.

Constructionist principle

Participants were explicitly asked to explore developments and struggle in self, relationship, and community and how they were affected by behaviour and attitudes (patterns lived and stories told), encouraging a reflexive consciousness about how reality gets made. The intention was to position participants to be conscious of a changing pattern lived and to learn about the conditions that made that possible.

Critical principle

The intervention drew attention to some habitual rules for interpreting the communications of others while questioning these *reflex* interpretations and inviting a more reflexive approach to choices when in the thick of communication. In proposing that all could hold optimism and pessimism, excitement and apprehension, the consultants warned against the tendency for qualities to get lodged in persons. In reflecting on this, it becomes possible for individuals to become curious about their own responses and to construct more "mindful" actions with community interests and purposes in mind.

The attitudes of the other were treated as a legitimate focus for commentary. At first, participants resisted this responsibility but the consultants held their ground and challenged this avoidance, arguing that the community had complained about the difficulty in holding on to their own learning. Here was an opportunity to practise giving feedback with compassion, humility, and generosity for the other. It was agreed that they go ahead and the feedback following was that the knowledge that all participants were taking this risk for the good of the community was liberating and healing.

Appreciative principle

The exercise was supportive of the claim that all action is meaning-ful, encouraging a purposeful inquiry into meaning and the making of connections between meanings. A deep appreciation was shown of the struggle and achievements in change.

Complexity principle

In drawing attention to the "uncharacteristic" intervention of the individual prior to the election, the consultants were exposing a critical transitional moment in the pattern development of the community. They shared the idea that the seeds for hope are in despair. This is a parallel idea to that of complexity theory that the seeds for change are where there is most noise in the system.

The *strange loop* provided a vehicle for healing the whole by showing how the fragmented parts connected. Circularity was also defined between the looped pattern and the contextual stories that held them in place.

Continuing the monks' tale

The benefits of a successful election, combined with the commu-nity's developing abilities to live reflexively in relationship to their own patterns, were apparent in the ways they were able to proceed with daily living, acting constructively in relation to the manage-ment of differences. In this context, we were asked to facilitate a discussion for the community about the future of the project that had been the focus for such demoralizing conflict, now some five years ago. Previously they had employed an outside profes-sional administrator to run the project, but since that person had left a member of the community had taken the responsibility for its running. It became clear to us, through initial discussion with the leader and a small commissioning group, that it would be unwise, and even unethical, to act as if it were possible to have the discussion about the project without also shining a direct light on feelings and thoughts about the relational issues that still existed. It was felt, by many, that insufficient reconciliation had been attempted by the community for the hurts imposed on particular people involved in the conflict at that time. It was conveyed that further work was needed if the community were to enact its responsibilities and accountabilities appropriately. However, there was also anxiety and concern expressed about raising these issues in a direct way. In particular, a fear was expressed that the substantive issues of the project that urgently needed discussion and decision would be hijacked by a relational focus. We consultants agreed to design a process that enabled both to be addressed.

Reflexive inquiry intervention

Stage 1: Constructing purpose

Individually reflect for a few minutes on the following:

By the time we have finished talking about this what would you like to have happened?

What ways of talking will help that and how might you participate?

Then turn to person next to you and share.

Then share in the group.

Stage 2: Learning: the story so far

Everyone addresses some questions in groups of three:

What are the important strengths and fragilities in the story of the project so far from your perspective? Why has it gone well and where is there shakiness of ground?

What might be the learning for this discussion?

Feedback and reflection.

Then back into small groups:

How do you view your responsibility, the community's and others' responsibility in what took place?

What is the community's responsibility and accountability now both for yourselves and for others who were affected?

Feedback and reflection.

Then in the light of what you've heard: What proposals might you want to make for progressing communication in the community around this and related issues?

Who if anyone might it be useful to contact and in relation to what?

Who should do the contacting and how should it be framed?

Feedback

Stage 3: Vision: the emerging story

Back in small groups:

How would you articulate purpose for the project that both expresses and develops the identity and purpose of the community?

In the light of that purpose what should the project be doing in terms of programmes and outreach and networks in broad terms?

What levels and mechanisms of involvement of the members of the community should there be in the organization, running and activities of the project?

Presentations back to large group with each grouping taking it in turns to sit at the centre with an extra 3 chairs provided for others, in response, to take positions of inquiry, challenge, support/development

Stage 4: Decision: realizing the story

Small groups work on distilling what they have heard. Under the 3 categories of organization, running and activity—distil what you think is the mind of the community—an individual from each group reports back.

Ownership: making the story our own

Reflections in plenary on relationship to the project now.

Revisiting RI principles

Systemic principle

The community showed an awareness that strategizing about the future of a core project could not occur without giving attention to its responsibilities for past behaviour in relation to the project and its personnel, but struggled with finding a way to achieve that in a way that the relational and the task could contextualize each other. The exercise allowed for that systemic connection, honouring the significance of both contexts.

Constructionist principle

It had become apparent that there was a felt need for the community to take action with regard to its responsibilities to others at the relational level. Meaning-making and change of relationship within the community was not enough. Consciousness had developed about how communication had positioned certain people as constrained actors in the real world and accountability for that positioning was articulated. The exercise enabled people to consider what their responsibilities should be, in the context of those of others.

Critical principle

It was articulated that the community *had done something wrong and then walked away*. The exercise enabled critique to occur at individual, relational, and group levels. It also facilitated progress rooted in critical action.

Appreciative principle

All views were treated as valid. The exercise stimulated the response of curiosity and concern towards the perspectives and feelings of those that were felt to have been hurt.

Complexity principle

The community showed through its ability in facing and handling these difficult issues, its growing consciousness and strength in managing complexity, in not splitting its responsibilities off, in not polarizing tensions and dilemmas. The exercise encouraged this ability through enabling a multi-faceted positioning in relation to the issues at community, relational, and identity levels.

Summary

Chapter Three has offered a case study incorporating three structured exercises of inquiry, intended to facilitate the development of reflexivity in a community's communication. In this case, participants came to see that a vocabulary for enacting new patterns of communication was needed and grew to develop that vocabulary over time through a persistent focus on the connection between feeling, meaning, and action and individual, relationship, and community. The frame of RI was shown to be invaluable in helping consultants enact their commitments, mindful of the ways their own communication provided opportunities and constraints for the progress of their clients.

Notes

1. Martin Daly, a systemic psychotherapist and consultant and himself a member of a religious order.
2. Rules for meaning and action in a system of communication (from Wittgenstein).

CHAPTER FOUR

Reflexive inquiry for organizational development

C hapter Four explores the relationship between content, structure, and process in the management of dialogue, at different levels of intervention and hierarchy, and with different sizes of group. This is explored through a description of organizational development work with a Christian mission organization (we will call it CMO) in London.[1] First, I connect an RI approach to working with groups with the wider literature of large group work, in particular that of future conferencing, a hybrid of future search and search conferencing (Ryan, 2004). Then I distil the principles of RI into some guidelines for designing structures for group dialogue. I go on to describe the aims, designs, and processes of four group events within the mission agency, one in greater detail than the others, to show the workings of RI in facilitating dialogue for organizational development with both large and small groups.

Future conferencing and RI

Future conferencing originated in the 1960s as a methodology for facilitating leadership decision-making and effectiveness, particularly in relation to strategic planning (Emery & Purser, 1993). The methodology has developed and is used internationally to facilitate the creation of effective proposals and plans for action in a variety of contexts. A future conference is "a method for enabling diverse groups of people to create a set of proposals or a plan based around their common future" (Emery & Purser, 1993, p. 2). It organizes small and large group discussions around a specific task and output. RI fits with this definition, in that it facilitates the development of plans for action through a process of collective meaning-making. However, its relationship to time will usually be more complex. The task will always be defined in the language of learning, for the purpose of facilitating future functioning, but may require a reflexive focus on the workings of the past in order to achieve that, whereas future conferencing, like AI, privileges a future focus. An RI focus will not necessarily be related to future corporate strategy but may be connected to a particular cultural theme, e.g., the development of leadership or team; the development of systems; or the management of relational boundaries.

Future conferencing draws on the work of Bion (1959) in designing structures and processes for dialogue. Bion's observation was that groups show an inclination to develop patterns of task avoidance. These patterns may show themselves through fight or flight behaviours, dependency on leader, and/or through sub-group formation. Future conferencing shares this hypothesis and works to ensure groups stay connected to task through locating power for design and decision-making in the group and through privileging the future as a focus. The emphasis is on a shift from what is called judgement thinking to design thinking (De Bono, 2003). With a connected but different emphasis, RI proposes that a group, in order to cooperate creatively, needs to believe that its task is purposeful and meaningful in the context of its wider obligations. The following guidelines have been developed to facilitate such cooperation.

Practical guidelines for RI and organizational development

Create a theme for the inquiry

A systemic sensibility helps us to understand the importance of creating a *gestalt*, or whole, that represents the coherence of the parts. It is my view that the title or theme of an organizational development process holds the potential for operating as an aesthetic container for the feelings, thoughts, and actions of participants in a process. The language and tone of a title will work as a context marker for the event, shaping opportunities and constraints for the episode itself and for identity, relationship, and cultural discourses. AI practitioners suggest that it is important to imagine what is being drawn attention to, in the language used to frame themes and subjects of inquiry. They resolve the struggle of definition by arguing that if you frame a theme in the language of problem you will create problem talk. The position taken here is that the title should be experienced as meaningful, invoke a sense of purpose and invite the potential for reflexive learning. The theme of struggle or ambiguity should not necessarily be avoided. However, it is important that the subject of inquiry should hold aspiration and motivation to work in the group for the group.

Facilitate the construction of stake and purpose

Participation in any organizational development process should ideally include those whose work affects and/or will be affected by the dialogue that occurs. Participants need to be able to give themselves an account of purpose for their presence that makes sense to them. It is important that the design of the dialogue enables this account to come into existence and to develop through the process.

Construct a dialogue that enables a balance of the domains of aesthetics, production and explanation

For Habermas (1970), the favoured discourse of rationality for many organizations is that of *instrumental reasoning*, privileging the world of facts and objectivity. This form of rationality can be thought of as occurring in the *domain of production*. So-called *practical reasoning*, which can be thought of as occurring in the *domain of explanation*, and privileges the exploration of patterns of meaning, is often either absent or marginalized, leading to a difficulty in creating shared meanings, and potentially undermining of morale. Of course, in some organizations, the tendency is for imbalance in favour of *practical reasoning*, leading to a struggle in decision-making.

An important dimension of the task of RI, whether in large or smaller groups, is to create a dialogue to provide an experience of balance, circular connectedness, and development. For balance, there needs to be an experience of opening up a subject, of making meaning and of punctuating the subject in relation to decision, an experience of closing down. However, it is also necessary to enable participants to create a reflexive relationship to the domains of explanation and production, in the domain of aesthetics, so that second order learning can be achieved about how to construct a process whereby shared meanings and decisions can be produced.

The circular connectedness of the dialogue is important in providing an experience of satisfied wholeness, not of fragmentation, so participants can be aware of when they are in which phase of the dialogue, and see and enact how each phase connects to the next, providing an experience of development. It is important that people leave the process being able to say *we got somewhere* and *we have a sense of where we might go next*. An account needs to be created about where, when, and how this dialogue fits with other organizational dialogues that have been and that are going to come.

AI practitioners use the 4D cycle, naming the four phases of dialogue as *discovery*, *dream*, *design*, and *delivery*. This does provide a balanced, connected, and developmental experience in the way described above, although it creates a particular kind of discursive closure through assuming what counts as negative and marginalizing it. There are many ways to fulfil the criteria described above. The practical examples that follow will show some possibilities.

Construct relational rules for participation

It is important that a coherent message is given at the levels of content and process about the relational and cultural expectations of the process. A sufficiently shared account needs to be created about the kind of communication that would be of value. Usually I would define the core element as reflexivity and frame it in three ways: that this is a group looking at itself; that the process will reinforce or change identities, relationships, and culture; it is thus important that what gets discussed and how it is discussed is done purposefully and with critical consciousness about what is being created through the ways people talk and listen. I usually invite agreement and inquire what else is important for participants to hold in mind through the process.

Coordinate rules for the talk

An important consideration here is *context* and the ability to know how to act within a context. Each context for dialogue that is set needs to offer clarity about purpose, positioning of identities, and entitlements and obligations in relationship. The relationships of significance are those: of participants to each other; of participants to the leadership of the process; and of participants to those implicated by the process but not present. Participants need to be sufficiently clear about their roles, purposes, tasks, and parameters of dialogue at each stage.

Structures for participation

The example here (Figure 12) is provided for literal or metaphorical use. This 4C cycle, an adaptation of the 4D cycle, uses words that connect etymologically to the word "critical" and are given to illustrate

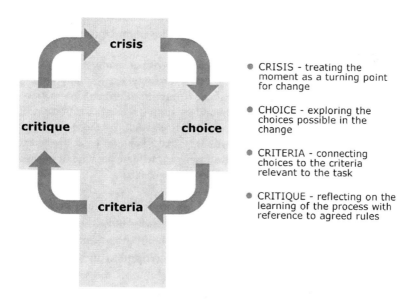

- CRISIS - treating the moment as a turning point for change

- CHOICE - exploring the choices possible in the change

- CRITERIA - connecting choices to the criteria relevant to the task

- CRITIQUE - reflecting on the learning of the process with reference to agreed rules

Figure 12.   The 4C cycle

the way a structure could work through opening, closing, and reflecting on the dialogue.

The Christian mission organization (CMO)

The leadership of the organization was keen to develop a culture, through organizational development, that facilitated the integration of the organizational and the spiritual. This cultural development would stimulate the realization of its vision through a mission strategy with a ten-year span. Key changes in senior personnel and a recent history of the opening up of participation in the development of vision had stimulated such desire for a review of strategy, leadership, structure, and culture. Mission strategy was seen as holding potential for combining the powers of intellect and ability in action, with love (for God and each other), spirituality, compassion, and service. This combination came to be called *mission spirituality*. However, organizational history showed, in its patterns of communication, that the meaning given to such words was contested and needed negotiation and definition.

An example of the kind of language used by the organization to convey its aims is represented by the following quote from its organizational development strategy. The organization

> aims to develop in a way that coheres with an understanding of I Corinthians 12, recognizing the interconnectedness and interdependence of its body. Human communication and interaction processes are felt to be key to understanding the organization, and, consequently, to managing change. It was felt, by those commissioning the work of the consultants, that RI should be at the heart of organization development strategy to facilitate the kind of meaning making and relational consciousness desired.

Leadership of the organization wanted its mission strategy to express new ways for engaging in mission; new relational structures; systemic forms of management development; an integration of the relational and the task; development in accountability structures and processes; clarity of rights and responsibilities for parameters and scope of participation; clarity of role and task expectations; and understanding of how the task of the individual fits with the primary task of the organization. As a consultant I was invited to participate in this process at many different levels. Some examples are: running a systemic management development pro-gramme over three years for all managers; developing identity, role, and task of board members; working at the boundary of relation-ship between board members and executive leadership; working at the boundary of relationship between senior and middle managers; facilitating team development; design and development of a new appraisal system; facilitation of a dialogue to develop a new system of pay and rewards; strategy development; development of the concept of relational leadership; facilitating the meaning of membership of the organization; and mentoring of individuals.

A working hypothesis for change

In our work with CMO we identified a cultural pattern that showed itself in episodes of communication creating experiences of dilemma, discomfort, and contradiction. This was a pattern of ambiguous accountability process and structure. It seemed to be shaped by a perceived and enacted polarization between manage-ment and the pastoral, which iterated in an either/or approach to care and critique. The split was indicated, for instance, through the ways that people at different levels of functional hierarchy called each other to account for their actions, showing, at times, a confu-sion about rights and responsibilities in what could and should be required, demanded, invited, requested. Some illustrations include: when middle management held a dialogue amongst themselves about their direction, their staff defined themselves as *excluded*, denying middle management the right to (temporarily) define issues that concerned themselves as a group. The response of middle management was to find it difficult to create a justifying account for their action and impossible to limit complaint. Another illustration is that it was not uncommon for some individuals to publicly define themselves as *non Christian* and unsupportive of the aims of the organization, but were not called to account for their behaviour. Another is that an appraisal system was in place but was underused as a vehicle for the management of performance and development.

    Challenge and critique were either treated as *unloving* acts or offered without a moment's thought about their effects. Confusion was shown about what counted as appropriate relational and task care and responsibility in the process of engaging in CMO work. Our sense was that the ability to give and receive feedback that held the necessary complexity of both support and challenge was compromised in this organization in a way that became very constraining. The organization had, thus far, experienced it as problematic to conduct a dialogue about what counted as appropriate care within the system's structures and processes and to discern how rights and responsibilities for care should be made accountable. One way of resolving the polarization was to widen the cultural (and spiritual) conception of management to incorporate appropriate relational care and responsibility.

We felt the key to making this integration might be to place the organizational function firmly as the highest context for action, but our hypothesis was that for CMO, *church as family* had developed as the overriding context giving meaning to action. *Church as family* would need to be treated as an important reference point but not higher than the organizational function. The primary function for a family could be said to be the individual care and growth of its members. However, we were prepared to propose that *the primary function of an organization should be the coordination of the efforts of its members to carry out its mission and task.*

In designing RI processes at different levels of relationship and task, we found the pattern shown in Figure 14 a useful orientating guide facilitating our intervention, encouraging the corporate to set a context for individual purpose and action and facilitating a sense for how the individual could shape organizational strategy.

We saw our task as consultants to be facilitating organizational episodes of accountable consultation, debate, instruction, and negotiation that made sense within organizational strategy, commitment, and purpose, and expressed appropriate authority and care for the relational within an integrated morally and functionally conscious management identity. The aim was to achieve maximum coherence of culture, relationship, and identity as levels of feeling, meaning, and action became mutually reinforcing over time with built-in processes and structures for reflexive learning.

RI approaches were thus used in a variety of ways at different levels of relationship and task. Four examples of RI design, including one example in detailed case study, follow.

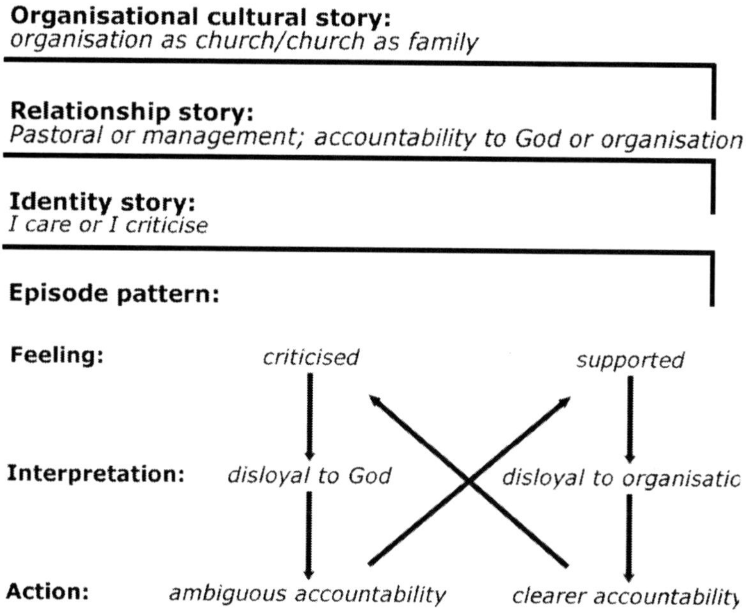

Organisational cultural story:
organisation as church/church as family

Relationship story:
Pastoral or management; accountability to God or organisation

Identity story:
I care or I criticise

Episode pattern:

Feeling: *criticised*   *supported*

Interpretation: *disloyal to God*   *disloyal to organisatic*

Action: *ambiguous accountability*   *clearer accountability*

Figure 13.   Problematic strange loop constructing ambiguous accountability

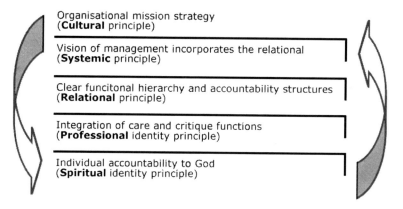

Organisational mission strategy
(**Cultural** principle)

Vision of management incorporates the relational
(**Systemic** principle)

Clear funcitonal hierarchy and accountability structures
(**Relational** principle)

Integration of care and critique functions
(**Professional** identity principle)

Individual accountability to God
(**Spiritual** identity principle)

figure 14.   Pattern facilitating clear accountability structures

Case study 1: Developing trustee role and relationship

Theme for inquiry

The non-executive trustee board of the organization had changed in its membership. Almost half of the group were new. Previous patterns of relationship and responsibility were felt by the Chair and the Chief Executive Officer (CEO) not to be fitting with the cultural development needed in CMO, and this new formation of membership was treated as an opportunity to develop role and relationship between trustees and between trustee group and executive group. The experience of Chair and CEO was that there had been a lack of clarity about appropriate boundaries of responsibility, with trustees taking up and being invited into working on operational issues rather than functioning at the strategic level. This confusion of role and accountability was felt to shape and be part of a general confusion of accountability in CMO. The group of twenty-five trustees and directors met for a day to work on the theme of *developing role and relationship*.

Facilitating construction of stake and purpose

The context for the work was set by the Chair who explicitly identified the need for the development of a greater culture of clarity in CMO about accountability, role, responsibility, relationship and reflexivity. He proposed that this introduction of RI to the trustees was part of that cultural change. He framed the inquiry as an opportunity to shape and build working practices and culture and explained how exercises had been designed to develop connection to the theme and commitment to the process of building role and relationship.

Constructing the dialogue to enable a balance of domains

The mnemonic ROLE was used to frame the dialogue. The R stood for *rationale*, the O for *opening*, the L for *listening* and the E for *emerging*. The use of a word to frame the dialogue like this seems to function as a container in the form of a pattern of letters, drawing attention to the key theme and providing the opportunity for opening, closing, and learning.

Coordinating rules for relational participation

The power, responsibility and accountability of the trustee group were emphasized. It was stressed that while the group would be working on the content of clarity of role and relationship and particular protocols for group functioning, it was also building relationship through the process. It was suggested that these early conversations in the life of the group would be particularly shaping of relational and group cultural patterns, so people were asked to show mindfulness about how that was done. Thus, a reflexive learning space was created so that process and content were developing in parallel.

Coordinating rules for task

The purpose and nature of the task at each stage of the dialogue was spelt out, with people given the opportunity to question and discuss their role, responsibility, and relationship within each task, thus constructing coherence between form and content at each point (see Figure 15).

Rationale: in pairs of director and trustee, with some observers, directors interviewed trustees for about twenty minutes, with reference to the core questions: *how does the trustee role express your values? What ideas does this create about your contribution to CMO?* Each pairing agreed on the four most significant points to feedback into the larger group.

Opening: In groups of three with the roles of interviewer, interviewee, and observer, an interview was conducted about key issues of role boundary. The trustee being interviewed was asked *what he or she was being called to do as a trustee*, imagining relevant stakeholders. The question next explored was: *what key relationships need building and how would they best work?* The feedback process was organized so that the interviewee group spoke in a public reflection first, then the interviewer group, then the observers. This form of feedback allowed people to speak from their position in the dialogue, giving due consideration to multiple perspectives and positions through a layering of reflection.

Listening: small groups worked on key protocols for the functioning and structuring of the trustee group and shared their work in plenary.

Emerging: a reflection in plenary occurred about the experience of working as a new trustee group and the benefits and constraints of the process for facilitating the work of the group.

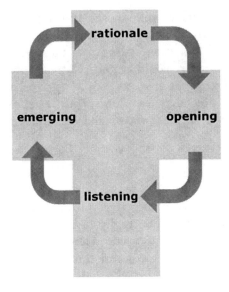

RATIONALE - Directors interview trustees. How does trustee role express their values? How to contribute? Feedback 4 most signigicant points

OPENING - groups of 3, interviewer, interviewee and observer; interview about key issues of role boundary; what are you called to do as trustee? What relationships need building and how would they work? Feedback from the 3 positions in groups

LISTENING - small groups work on key protocols; share 3 points

EMERGING - learning and critique of process

Figure 15. Structure for participation

Case study 2: Developing a new appraisal system

Theme for inquiry

All staff of CMO (approximately one hundred people) came together to develop a dialogue about the shape of a new appraisal system for CMO. Appraisal was defined as a core management tool for the review, development, and management of performance in the context of mission strategy. The aim of the work for the consultants was to create an experience of engaged participation in the process of definition and purpose of an appraisal system with the effect that participants would develop individual commitment to its working and make sense of its place in the wider endeavour of mission strategy.

The consultants set their working context by calling the event a *critical appreciative inquiry into appraisal.* There was a conscious attempt here to encourage the expression of critical appreciation and appreciative criticism in the communicative processes of the organization. The word "critical" was deconstructed into the words *crisis, choice, criteria,* and *critique.* These words were used in both setting the context and structuring the dialogue.

The construction of stake and purpose

The personnel department had set up a working group representative of different interests and levels of organizational hierarchy. The head of personnel publicly framed the aim for this event to be influencing the design of the appraisal system through an exploration of staff's experience of appraisal from the past and aspirations for the future. The CEO set a context by connecting the theme of accountability with the spiritual.

The consultants used the word *crisis* to invoke the sense of opportunity that this turning point offered for staff to shape the future of organizational practice in a meaningful way. The aims were defined as enhancing the connection between individual performance and mission strategy; between performance and development; and between valuing the work and feeling valued.

Constructing dialogue to allow for a balance of domains

The cycle of *crisis, choice, criteria,* and *critique* (detailed below) enabled the balance of focus and development of dialogue required to create an opening up and closing down process, incorporating reflexive learning.

Rules for relational participation

We invited participants into a position of treating the use of language as a turning point and to consider that they had *choice* in the ways they expressed their experience, learning, and hopes for the future. We suggested that the organization is made through the ways it communicates to itself. In reflecting on *choice*, we proposed that the *criteria* used should be meaningful and purposeful and facilitate mutual accountability to mission strategy. We proposed a relational learning process following the development of ideas about appraisal.

Coordinating rules for the task

Each phase of the dialogue was carefully constructed so that participants were clear as to why, what, and how they should be speaking and listening. It was obvious that this cycle of dialogue would shape the design task of the working group. Timings for completion of task and parameters of responsibility were given (see Figure 16).

Crisis: Groups of eight discussed their experience about appraisal—both effective and fragile experiences—and explored their learning about the conditions for the effective and fragile experience. Out of this experience they were invited to define one bold goal for future appraisal processes. The goals were fed into plenary and put in context of resonant experiential themes.

Choice: Groups of four took the proposal from the working party on appraisal and worked on the proposal, feeding into plenary.

Criteria: This work developed in the next phase where people were asked to reflect on what they had heard and to consider what should be taken and used from people's ideas that would allow an appraisal process that would enhance mission strategy. The presentation of these ideas was invited in the form of a news page of a daily newspaper—the "Daily Appraiser". This intervention was aimed to encourage metaphorical and creative thinking in ways that distilled the best of ideas and presented them in a concrete form.

Critique: the working group reflected in public on the presentations and responded to questions from the floor about their

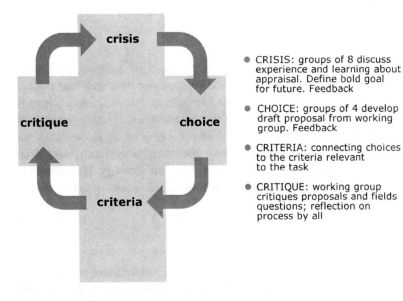

● CRISIS: groups of 8 discuss experience and learning about appraisal. Define bold goal for future. Feedback

● CHOICE: groups of 4 develop draft proposal from working group. Feedback

● CRITERIA: connecting choices to the criteria relevant to the task

● CRITIQUE: working group critiques proposals and fields questions; reflection on process by all

Figure 16. Structure for participation

responses and how they might act in relation to them. Finally there was a reflection amongst the group of one hundred on the process and what had been created through the dialogue.

Case study 3: Strategic planning and reflexive inquiry

Theme for inquiry

The inquiry was entitled *CMO leaders' residential: a reflexive inquiry*. Senior and middle managers had a pattern of meeting every year to engage in strategic planning for the year ahead in the context of long and medium term goals of mission strategy. On this occasion, they met for three days to develop agreements for operationalizing strategy. My role as consultant was to facilitate a reflexive inquiry into the workings of each day so that both content and process could be given appropriate attention. An hour was given to the reflexive inquiry at the end of each day.

Facilitating construction of stake and purpose

The CEO set a context for the three days with the words: *paradigm, plan*, and *pruning* (3Ps). He made clear how important it was for content and relational process to be given attention. Then senior managers responsible for different departments updated the group about key review processes. This included financial strategy and position and personnel implications.

Constructing a dialogue enabling a balance of domains

For the main part of each day the group worked on its plan and, as consultant, I observed the process. In a spirit of coherence I chose 4Ps to frame the evening dialogue. I used the words, *partial, political, purposeful*, and *positioning*. The balance that was important to construct here was that between the part and the whole: of individual consciousness of their own interests; how they connected to those of others; and how they shaped those of others in the market place of strategy negotiation.

Coordinating rules for relational participation

The 4Ps were also used to construct relational rules at the outset of the three days and an attempt was made to express the grammar of the organizational and spiritual. The word *partial* was used to draw attention to three other words. People were asked if they were prepared to show: humility: I suggested that from our human position we see an incomplete picture: vulnerability: I advocated that people be prepared for openness to change through engagement with others; open-handedness; I encouraged working for the good of the whole.

The word *political* was used to draw attention to how, at a relational level, we were coordinating and grappling with issues and interests for the sake of CMO as *church*. It was suggested that this process would create developments, dilemmas, and tensions. I wanted to give permission for all reactions to be experienced but to invite people into a reflexive responsibility in relation to them. Hence, I used the word *positioning* to propose that through the discussions we would be in a flow of creating opportunities and constraints for ourselves, and others, in taking up purposes, positions and interests. I concluded by proposing that, together, we were building CMO as church and that *purposeful*, constructive contributions would enable that to be an effective process. Hence, the 4Ps were used to frame the relational process as well as the task process.

Coordinating rules for task

This task was to be juxtaposed with, and understood in relation to, the task of developing strategy. This explicit task, however, was to consider the relational process. Exercises were designed in each phase of the dialogue to facilitate clarity about task in relation to the 4Ps as themes. In cross-department groups people discussed four questions for fifteen minutes (see Figure 17).

Partial: First, in small cross department groups, people explored what had helped them to show openness in the dialogue.

Political: Second, people explored the dilemmas and tensions in content and process and how they were relating to them.

Positioning: Third, they explored how they were, as individuals, inviting and constraining others in the dialogue and how that could be done differently.

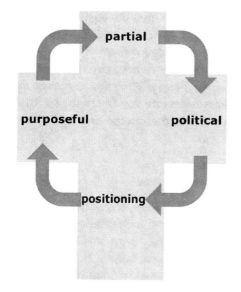

- PARTIAL - what has helped and constrained us to show openness in the dialogue?

- POLITICAL - what are the tensions and dilemmas in content and process and how are we relating to them?

- POSITIONING - how are you inviting and constraining others in the process? How could you do it differently?

- PURPOSEFUL - what is the learning from today that you want to take into tomorrow?

Figure 17. Structure for participation

Purposeful: Fourth, they explored what the learning might be from the day's dialogue and how they might want to shape it tomorrow.

In plenary they shared key points, mindful of how the feedback contributed to the building of CMO. This was followed by free reflections in the large group.

Case study 4: Relational leadership at the edge of chaos

Theme for inquiry

The words *relational leadership* had been used by the organization over time as if they represented shared meaning, but the notion had never been explored corporately. The organization was facing a time in its life when radical change was imposed through financial constraint, creating an anxiety about disintegration. Review and change in policy, process, procedure, and personnel was under way and the Directors' group felt that a time for reflexive reflection about the relational impact on processes of leadership within their own group was necessary to encourage corporate and individual confidence in the process with which they were engaged.

The *edge of chaos* was invoked to convey how the creative potential in an organization is at the place of *bounded instability*—neither a place of order or disorder but on the edge of both. This approach invites attention to the relational conditions necessary for organizational creativity at times of change (Stacey, 2000) and proposes that the kind of relational conditions necessary for creativity are those that build reflection and learning into strategic and operational activity.

Facilitating construction of stake and purpose

The aims of the work were developed with representatives from the Directors' group, as being to: offer a model for exploring the experience of *relational leadership* in practice; create more understanding in the group about individuals' experience of connectivity, diversity, responsiveness, power, and anxiety, key factors identified as mediating of relational dynamics (Stacey, 2000); and develop a corporate potential of *relational leadership at the edge of chaos*.

Diversity was defined at the level of experience and perspective. It was proposed that it can be useful to treat all communication as potentially cross-cultural, thus encouraging conditions for curiosity and empathy. *Connectivity* was defined as the ability to connect with others even though one may not share a perspective or experience. It was proposed that the ability of people to show *responsiveness* is challenged when it is either hard to make sense of someone else's behaviour or when too much sense is made of it and assumptions rigidified. The challenge becomes more acute when motives are maligned and language becomes linear, for instance, *you did this to me*. It was suggested that the relevance of *power* to the relational in this context is in the refinement of consciousness about the effects of people's influence on each other, whether peers or subordinates and people's abilities to use power in a balanced way. The containment of *anxiety* (one's own and that of others) is treated as a core function of leadership in these terms.

Constructing a dialogue enabling a balance of domains

The dialogue was divided into four elements. The first was focused on individual experience of leadership; the second, building on learning from the first, on group relational patterns; the third on organizational action; the fourth on reflexive learning. This layering enabled movement between exploring and learning about individual experience and reflection on group process and deciding on organizational action.

Coordinating rules for relational participation

Participants were encouraged to notice and reflect on their own process and how it expressed *relational leadership*. They were also encouraged to support and challenge each other's contributions through the dialogue structure.

Coordinating rules for task

Each phase had distinct rules of operation, encouraging the sharing of and responding to observations at the individual, group and organizational levels.

Structure and process for participation

Individual experience

Each person spent five minutes alone, reflecting on the following questions:

- What does relational leadership mean to you?
- What are significant hopes and challenges for you with reference to key relational factors of connectivity, diversity, responsiveness, power and anxiety?
- What support and challenge do you need from the leadership group to help you in your leadership task?

Each person then, in turn, gave a response to the questions, while others listened and then were invited to inhabit a position of *support, inquiry,* or *challenge*. These positions were allocated concrete space in the room, on particular chairs, where people were invited to place themselves when they wanted to speak.

Group relational patterns

Small groups reflected on themes and patterns, noting the unsaid as well as what was focused on.

Organizational action

Small groups developed proposals for action at individual, group, and corporate levels and wrote one on each card. Individual directors took responsibility for making a case for each proposal. If a colleague thought there was need for inquiry, development, or challenge of a proposal, they took the card up and offered their response in the next round of discussion. Agreements and disagreements were identified and decisions made about disposal of proposals.

Reflexive reflection

Discussion occurred about the workings of relational leadership in the group. As consultant I shared my own observations, using the structure of the relational conditions for *bounded instability* offered above.

Connectivity was shown through the levels of challenge and support that people offered. The dialogue was enhanced when people took risks and asked difficult questions or showed vulnerabilities previously unknown. The theme of insiders–outsiders emerged in relation to: experiences and stories of marginalization; jealousy about different resources and positions; disconnections over the use of language; involvement or the lack of it in decision-making. The question of whom should be involved in any decision, conversation, project, and how, is perhaps a particular sensitivity that needs addressing at times of change.

Cross-cultural *diversity* had been raised as both a value and a challenge. Some members felt themselves to be outside the cultural norms of the group; others experienced differences in perspective about models of leadership. It occurred to me that this could be a useful focus for further exploration in the group. Where do people most experience difference? Where is it explicit and where implicit? Where is it of value? Where is it problematic?

The theme of absence and presence was developed in relation to *responsiveness*. It caused me to reflect on what dialogues needed to occur between members of the group and with staff so that the image of the *good enough* leader or colleague is held, even when the physicality is absent.

Power was shown to be a contested site in this group. The hypothesized effect on patterns of interaction was that some perspectives went underground and emerged in an unwanted and unplanned way. The group explored cases where dilemmas or conflicts in relation to power had emerged. This was felt to be an uncomfortable process, but also clarifying where there were misunderstandings, agreements, disagreements, and unintended impact on others.

In relation to the theme of *anxiety*, I observed different levels of openness and defensiveness and noticed (not surprisingly) that openness invited risk-taking and development of the dialogue and defensiveness created a situation where it was difficult to ask questions, as if there was no room for manoeuvre.

It appeared that this was a time where anxiety about loss and hurt were in evidence. I sensed reluctance in the group to identify in concrete terms where the losses and pains were. I proposed that the challenge for leadership might be how to maintain a balance of robustness and sensitivity to the experiences of others and enable purposeful discussion about the implications of change, while also steering it. This arguably required a specific focus on reflexive dialogue at different levels of hierarchy, incorporated into operational planning.

Summary

In this chapter I have shown how an RI approach can be used for organizational development at different levels of intervention. While these case examples express differences in content, structure, and process, the core principles of RI are employed as reference points for guiding design, meaning-making, and action. The organization described made a commitment to RI principles in its development of organizational culture and structure. This commitment provided a special opportunity for consultancy work and is suggestive of the importance of collaboration at levels of principle and practice between organizational leadership and consultant. Through this coordination, unwanted patterns at levels of culture, relationship, and identity were explored and problematized, while experiences of new patterns lived were offered through mindful design of organizational dialogue. The polarization of care and critique became unnecessary in the context of a more systemic critical appreciation shown in management practice through the systems and processes cultivated over time. Coordination of efforts in carrying out the organization's mission and task became more coherent.

Note

1.   Much of the work with this mission agency has been undertaken with a consultant colleague, Graham Brittain.

PART III

REFLEXIVE INQUIRY AS A QUALITATIVE RESEARCH TOOL

CHAPTER FIVE

Constructing a research lens for reflexive inquiry

T his chapter proposes that the ability to define a phase of consultancy as *research* will enable a different culture of investigation with concomitant differences in the entitlements and obligations that follow from this framing of purpose. Framing a phase of the work as research allows the task to be explicitly defined as making meaning and constructing learning. This can be of significant value, particularly when the consultant is working in an organizational culture driven by *instrumental reasoning* (Habermas, 1970).

I set a context for research as a tool in a consultancy process through locating the principles of RI within the language game of qualitative research and, in particular, a critical research tradition (Alvesson, 2003; Alvesson & Deetz, 2000; Alvesson & Skoldberg, 2000; Habermas, 1970). A research process will then be described that uses the principles to make sense of organizational patterns in a way that facilitates new action for a leadership group. The definition of the research task that best reflects the spirit of RI comes from the critical research tradition expressed by Alvesson and Deetz (2000). They define the research task as a complex interplay between the development of *insight* (interpretation of the local), *critique* (investigating the local through connecting micro practices and macro discourses), and *transformation* (connecting insight to social action). As will be seen in previous chapters, an incorporation of the critical tradition within RI renders some dimensions of the critical *voice* more visible, others more hidden, while yet others are transformed, for instance in the development of the notion of second- and third order critique.

The focus in a qualitative research context is, of course, to explore the meaning of social phenomena, not to count instances or make claims about frequencies (Silverman, 2000). However, Alvesson (2003, p. 30) points out that "there are not many efforts to develop a theoretical frame to understand context issues". He also suggests that it would be innovative to provide studies that combine *critical* and *non-critical* perspectives. Such an approach would be "even more novel, minimise the risk of hyper-critique and open up a possibility for reducing the gap between critical and conventional management studies" (Alvesson, 2003, p. 183). It is proposed here that an RI research approach can offer a structure for interpreting a complexity of contexts, perspectives, and interests.

I would argue strongly that it is important to employ theoretical frames for structuring interpretation in research or one runs the risk of taking up one-dimensional, fragmented and/or naïve positions. Alvesson (2003) has recently advocated accessing a variety of metaphors as frames for interpreting the same empirical material, proposing the importance of the researcher developing a familiarity with a span of vocabularies and theories as an aid to reflexivity.[1] For him, reflexivity in research terms shows itself as "an interpretive, open, language sensitive, identity conscious, historical, political, local, non authoritative and textually aware understanding of the subject matter" (Alvesson & Deetz, 2000, p. 113).

In his use of metaphor he is less concerned with a precision map but more interested to stimulate the production of ideas. Where his eight frames are: *construction, identity, cultural script, basic assumptions, politics, moral story telling or impression management, discourse,* and *local accomplishment,* mine will be the more abstract metaphors of *systemic, constructionist, appreciation, critical,* and *complexity.* These frames contain many of Alvesson's reference points, for example, identity, cultural script, but are organized so that these structures for interpretation are connected to particular commitments that facilitate reflexivity, both in the research process and as an outcome of the research. It will be suggested that when a researcher relates to their empirical material from these positions, the light thrown on the material will generate a sufficiently complex picture, to justify a credible research position and to provide a platform for local learning and transformation.

An RI commitment in a research language game necessitates linkage between interpretation and action. A key value of a critical research lens is that it enriches possibilities for those of us committed to reflexive methodologies in that it aims to reduce pre-structured limitations of feeling, thinking, and action that may be less visible to consciousness but are shown in patterns of sameness and variation (Alvesson, 2000). It explicitly and unashamedly positions the researcher as a change agent in balancing forms of *rationality* characterizing such pre-structuring. An example of pre-structuring might be a constraining discourse of *instrumental reasoning* (Habermas, 1970). The researcher might identify micro-moments of *instrumental reasoning* and connect them to macro patterns of culture at an organizational level. Working with an RI commitment, the development of reflexive agency for participants would be an explicit aim.

RI principles as interpretive metaphors

Systemic principle

A systemic frame provides a relational vocabulary for facilitating openness to complex patterns of meaning and action. In its focus on social and linguistic processes it allows the researcher to address something non-obvious (non-linear) and to make sense of it by making a *contextual gestalt,* connecting the parts to the whole. The systemic tradition can sit comfortably with a variety of *units of meaning* for interpretation. For instance, *patterns lived, narratives* or *stories told, micro* and *macro discourses.* An example might be an investigation of how acts of *micro power* could be connected to show how they fit with a broader discourse at the cultural or societal level. The *unit of meaning* that best fits one's purposes will emerge out of a complex interplay between theoretical frame, methods for generating empirical material, for instance, interview structures, and the empirical material itself. From a systemic lens, it is understood that the questions asked will shape the responses given, which will shape interpretive content. In this sense, it is necessary to keep returning to purpose and audience to assist in framing methodologies and to appreciate the circular nature of the research process. Choices and actions at each stage will encourage or discourage coherence between the parts and reflexivity in relation to them.

The interview as a form for generating meaningful material is a familiar phenomenon in a systemic frame, with its store of systemically motivated questions to facilitate the making of connections. The researcher is sensible to the interventive consequences of questions that reframe linear realities systemically, both for interviewee and interviewer. For instance, a researcher interested in the connection between power and voice in an organization might explore the process of a meeting by asking research participants:

> What were your observations about who spoke most in the meeting?
>
> How do you explain the pattern of voices?
>
> What relationships encourage or discourage such patterns?
>
> What did you notice about the effects of the ways voices were used on decisions that were taken?

Her purpose in exploring the connection between power and voice might be to investigate and create reflexivity about experiences of participation in the context of a description of poor organizational effectiveness or coherence.

Even though, from a systemic perspective, we need to take the view that there is not a 1:1 match of reality to interpretation, this does not mean interpretation is pointless. We need to be aware of how interpretive acts are constructed and consider how we shape these constructions. In these terms, the relationship between the researcher and her data is problematized in a research context, just as the systemically informed consultant will appreciate that her own assumptions and behaviour have influence on the patterns she is examining and engaging with. For instance, the researcher may, from her experience, believe that gender discourses play a core part in organizational participation. She would work to identify the operation of such assumptions and to imagine counter assumptions, and may use them as a resource for hypothesizing but attempt to be open to alternatives to her own assumptions in the empirical material, searching for the gender biases that are "not there" as well as those that are "there".

Constructionist principle

For the constructionist, people, realities, and relationships became contested complex constructions. This position forms the basis for interpretation. Reality is socially constructed with language (verbal and non-verbal) as a core component of that construction. The constructionist will examine a text for the contexts that create the text and the contexts created by the text. The special emphasis I bring to the constructionist lens, connected to a concern of critical theory and informed by CMM (Pearce, 1994), is an interest in how stories of obligation and entitlement at levels of organizational culture, relationship, and identity construct and are constructed by structures of feeling, meaning, and action.

Returning to the example about power and voice, we might find one circular narrative as:

Cultural story: insufficiently shared vision for contextualizing obligations and entitlements. Ability to contribute thus becomes over identified with structural position or individual ability rather than connected to shared purpose and clarity of rights and responsibilities to participate

Relational story: powerful/powerless

Identity story: my voice is not heard

Episode: staff meeting

Interpretive act: feeling: powerless

interpretation: I cannot contribute

action: lack of engagement

It would be important to expose alternative positions within the overall pattern to demonstrate the power-filled nature of the

discourse and its ramifications. It might also be important to identify a discourse of rationality, in Habermas's terms, thus facilitating
an experience of the power of discourse and, paradoxically, an
empowerment in relation to discourse.

Critical principle

For the critical researcher there is a concern about patterns of communication that prevent people acting in their own interests. The
focus for critique is *constraint and interest; communicative distortion;
frozen meanings; fixation of subjectivity; domination of discourses; lost
possibilities for action* (Alvesson & Deetz, 2000). This lens can provide
a direction and focus for an exploration of the relationship between
context and text. However, in the critical literature the critical position can be one-sided and *first order*. For instance, the focus very
often becomes the *imperfections of management*. An RI commitment
would insist on the incorporation of self-critique; the inclusion of
self as part of a pattern of oppression or asymmetry.

There is a sense in which all research should show critical
consciousness, in that no research claims should be accepted or
made without the researcher accounting for their contexts. Such
accounts should allow the process of linking concepts, methodologies, empirical material, and interpretation to be made visible and
transparent. Alvesson & Deetz (2000) suggest four practices for
facilitating such consciousness: identifying and challenging
assumptions beyond "ordinary" perceptions, conceptions, actions;
recognizing the influence of social, political, historical, and cultural
contexts on beliefs and actions; exploring alternatives that may
disrupt established patterns and routines and; distrusting any claim
that is said to express the truth and disallow alternatives.

In relation to our example, the researcher might examine the text
(transcript) of a meeting for *lost possibilities for action*. For instance,
if we treat the interpretive act in communication as an opportunity
or an invitation to engage, we will respond differently than if we
treat it as an attack or a disqualification or an attempt at closure.
The researcher could draw attention to those moments where
particular interpretations were made that constrained effective
communication and perhaps use this learning from the consultancy
position to create a vocabulary of alternatives. An example might

be where a participant in the meeting speaks passionately about his views but it is interpreted as displaying anger by others and argued with. His passionate intervention could have been treated as an invitation to explore the context for his passion but the patterned response (possibly well established) showed itself as competitive or symmetrical (Pearce, 1989) and closed down a developmental dialogue.

Appreciative principle

The appreciative principle in the context of RI alerts us to the dangers of treating any position as uncontested or as a grand narrative. In its emphasis on the multiply motivated and interpreted nature of experience, it would support a critical position in warning how *discursive closure* may exist wherever potential expression of difference or conflict is suppressed. Given the appreciative position that all action is meaningful, this perspective can help us to consider how unwanted patterns of action or conflict filled stories expressed by research participants may make sense in the context of organizational practices of *discursive closure*; for example, reflecting limited access to legitimate speaking forums (Alvesson & Deetz, 2000).

For instance, an AI organizational development process about experiences of participation, initiated by management, might effect *discursive closure* in its requirement to be positive. Such *discursive closure* may or may not be useful. What is advocated in an RI research context is an appreciation of the potential effects and purposes of the openings and closures that we create through communication. *Discursive invitation* is of equal interest to *discursive closure*. Neither is intrinsic to a communication. It might be most relevant to explore how interpretations of *discursive closure* could be transformed into *discursive invitation*.

Developing our example about power and voice, within an appreciative frame, it would be legitimate to facilitate the expression of concerns, doubts, hopes, and fears about participation—those that are difficult to express or be allowed expression, and for their identification to be linked to processes of *discursive closure* and *discursive invitation*.

Alvesson & Deetz (2000) have pointed out some of the patterns that can lead to *discursive closure*. These patterns can usefully frame the interpretive process. First, arrangements can be articulated in such a way that there is an experience of the *naturalization of social order*. If this pattern is prevalent, it feels self evident that the way processes work are not based on choice but the *natural* way for things to be. Second, *sectional interests* such as managerial interests can be treated as the interests of all parties and conflicting interests suppressed, not necessarily intentionally. A research process can help to highlight how *interest articulation* works. Third, *instrumental reasoning*, with its anti inquiry emphasis, can dominate and lay claim to rationality (Habermas, 1984) with the effect of loss of meaning and, thus, loss of staff motivation. Fourth, what Wilmott (1993, p. 534) calls *hegemony consent* can become orchestrated, whereby the conditions for the development of critical reflection are not fostered. It is not argued here that such processes would be strategically created but more that self (organizational) defeating patterns and routines can be established that may be, through a partial and fragmented lens, perceived as interest based, and their articulation could facilitate the development of organizational consciousness and agency.

An RI perspective enriches the language of *discursive closure* in adding *discursive invitation* as a potential reframing. While agency can be enhanced in facilitating an identification of unwanted patterns (*discursive closure*) it can arguably be enhanced still further in facilitating an identification of lost possibilities for *discursive invitation* in the ways that *interpretive acts* are being defined.

Complexity principle

While a critical approach in isolation would aim to reclaim conflict and fragmentation and disrupt the existing social order, an RI approach would emphasize more the development of consciousness and choice about access to and use of discourse and the interests that shape discourse. Its aim would be to show the partiality and complexity of reality and to help people locate themselves in that reality. Critical theory talks in terms of the ongoing task for organizational participants of *struggle* and *decision*. In my view it is probably helpful to think in these terms and to use *struggle* and *decision* as frames to alert ourselves as researchers to organizational complexity. The *strange loop* represents an embodiment of struggle and decision in the way it presents polarization and fragmentation as challenges to coherent decision-making. Other patterns such as charmed (virtuous) and hexed (vicious) loops (Oliver, Herasymowych, & Senko, 2003) can also be useful as interpretive tools in the articulation of complexity. While the charmed loop is one that incorporates reflexivity into its feeling, interpretation, and action cycle, the hexed loop is characterized by mistrust, pessimism, competition, and powerlessness.

Note

1. I follow Alvesson in his use of the words "empirical material" rather than data, encouraging a decoupling of the material and the interpretive process.

CHAPTER SIX

The peace builders' story: a problem of strategic coherence

I was charged as a consultant with facilitating leadership development in a non-governmental organization (NGO) working with violent conflict in *neglected war areas*. In talking to the senior management team I discovered that the organization itself had become a *neglected war area*. Staff had written to senior management complaining about lack of management support and pleading that they be managed. People felt demoralized and incompetent at all levels, although there was a lot of energy *out in the field* for working with conflict. My task was defined as developing management skill at the level of the individual manager and development of management culture for the organization.

My input was structured in the following way:

- research a *needs assessment* of management practice by interviewing the fourteen managers;
- present the findings to the management group as a basis for a management development dialogue over two days;
- conduct a management learning day with all staff, sharing the outcome of previous work and create a research inquiry into experiences and future possibilities for management practice;

- offer six further days of management development training for the managers

The individual managers were interviewed using the loosely structured interview protocol below:

- what would you say are the core management tasks in your work?;
- how do you evaluate your own performance of those tasks (address team work here and other core tasks)?;
- what would key others say about your performance?;
- describe an episode where you would say you were showing effective management;
- describe an episode showing the need for development;
- how do your ideas about management fit with the culture(s) and practices of the organization?;
- what culture(s) and practices facilitate/constrain your management task?;
- what would you say are your rights, responsibilities, obligations and entitlements as a manager?;
- where is there clarity about role and where need for clarity?;
- when do you feel most/least empowered?;
- what relationship patterns (e.g., collaborative, consultative, competitive) facilitate/constrain your management task?;
- where do patterns of information sharing and decision making work well/need development in the organization?;
- where are the similarities and differences between your conception of management and others in the organization?;
- what needs to be preserved/changed in the ways that management is understood and practised?;
- what should be the core tasks of a management development programme for the organization?;
- how would you wish to be practising differently as a manager if it were a successful programme?;
- how might such a programme affect the management/organizational culture of the organization?

These questions were designed to access *systemic* connections between meaning and action at the levels of organizational and management culture, management relationships, management style and skill, and the detail of episodes of performance. On transcribing the empirical material, key phrases were highlighted that were suggestive of the *construction* of moral obligation or entitlement, person position, or emotional tension at different levels of context; e.g., *it's not possible to criticize the line manager* was categorized as of interest at a relational level of context and an example of *discursive closure*. From a *critical* perspective, I looked for how *subjectivities were fixated, sectional interests,* and for *lost possibilities for action* or, in *appreciative* terms, *discursive invitation*. I also looked, from a *complexity* perspective, for *constraining discourses* and *patterns of fragmentation*. These frames for interpretation were selected from an RI repertoire as best fitting my initial hypothesizing about this organization's practices and processes. In the commissioning of the work, I observed that senior management told a story about wanting to create an effective organization with high staff morale, but were aware that unwanted management/staff patterns had developed over time. I made the researcher assumption that enhanced reflexivity about micro management practices and macro discourses could facilitate more aesthetic patterns.

The decision to present my "findings" in strange loop form was stimulated by the observation that the material showed oscillation, polarization, conflict, constraint, a lack of stability, and a lack of progress in struggle and decision. The looped patterns were presented as *systemic* forms of *discursive closure* and as opportunities for *discursive invitation*. Four themes stood out as of significance and meaningful material was clustered within these themes in the form of strange loops. The themes selected were: *strategic coherence; accountability; trust and fairness; appraisal.*

Strategic coherence

Quotes from data

We need to make the organization more professional.

We have no agreed frame for management.

There is leadership but you don't necessarily see it where you expect it.

We need to be able to say no to things with reference to the whole.

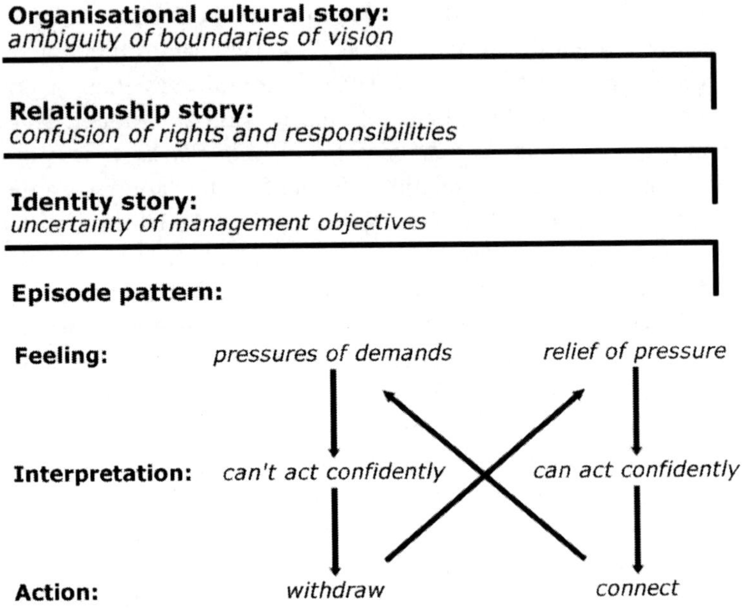

Organisational cultural story:
ambiguity of boundaries of vision

Relationship story:
confusion of rights and responsibilities

Identity story:
uncertainty of management objectives

Episode pattern:

Feeling: *pressures of demands*   *relief of pressure*

Interpretation: *can't act confidently*   *can act confidently*

Action: *withdraw*   *connect*

Figure 18.   Strategic coherence

Senior management make demands without looking into the detail—analysing the cost benefit.

Each team could all be a separate NGO.

The middle managers don't connect with each other.

No vehicles for middle managers to come together.

We don't exchange information effectively.

We don't actively make choices about what we should and shouldn't be doing—so overburdened.

Everything is regarded as propositional—decisions are often accidental and ad hoc.

Accountability

Quotes from data

We need structures that bind people to shared responsibility.

It's been an attempt to exert central control without understanding.

Organisational cultural story:
accountability not integrated with vision

Relationship story:
either/or: management or implementation; centre or field

Identity story:
accountable to local not the whole

Episode pattern:

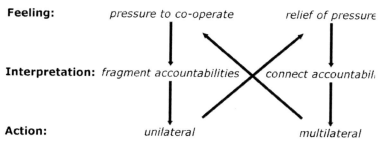

Feeling: *pressure to co-operate*   *relief of pressure*

Interpretation: *fragment accountabilities*   *connect accountabil,*

Action: *unilateral*   *multilateral*

Figure 19.   Accountability

We work most effectively by doing our own thing.

There is a link between funding and autonomy—we have to fund ourselves at the local level

there is no pay back in creating more connection.

Good management would look like: clear mutual expectations, regular weekly update, clear conditions for meeting goals, clarity about how the relationship works, an idea how I'm getting on against objectives.

We need more constructive consultation not nominal consultation.

Trust and fairness

Quotes from data

Leadership is afraid of expressing preferences at the level of vision and this creates inequality.

A safe space has not been created for all to give opinions.

It's not possible to criticize the line manager.

Organisational cultural story:
individual priotised over corporate

Relationship story:
inconsistency/inequity of treatment of staff

Identity story:
favoured/unfavoured

Episode pattern:

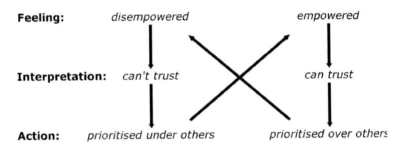

Feeling:	*disempowered*	*empowered*
Interpretation:	*can't trust*	*can trust*
Action:	*prioritised under others*	*prioritised over others*

Figure 20.   Trust and fairness

A culture of guilty until proven innocent.

We have never lifted the lid off cultural identity.

There is a real lack of trust and dissatisfaction at all levels particularly lower levels around inconsistent unfair treatment—despite the work that's been done.

People sometimes go outside proper procedures.

One person can be kept happy without thinking of fairness for the organization.

People sometimes have been promoted to management without a formal procedure.

There is not enough transparency about processes.

There is no pattern of personal discipline.

There is an "if you scratch my back I will scratch yours" opportunism—not looking at the good of the whole.

It's up to individual negotiation rather than fairness across the board.

Appraisal

Quotes from data

We need to devise mechanisms for listening and tolerating various perspectives.

There is a lack of stability because people are not present.

There is a difficulty in evaluating the work of each other—always a suspicion about common criteria.

Appraisal processes and procedures do not allow for a reality based assessment.

No time or systems to reflect on what we are learning.

This organization doesn't recognize the value of facilitative management.

I am frequently frustrated by the quality of support I get.

There is no real interest, support or relationship building.

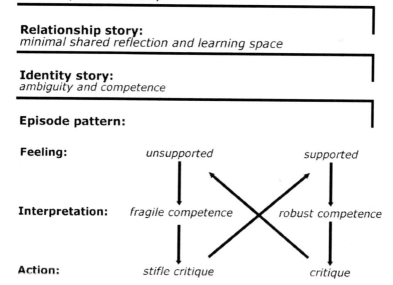

Organisational cultural story:
instability and insecurity

Relationship story:
minimal shared reflection and learning space

Identity story:
ambiguity and competence

Episode pattern:

Feeling:	*unsupported*	*supported*
Interpretation:	*fragile competence*	*robust competence*
Action:	*stifle critique*	*critique*

Figure 21.   Appraisal

A feeling of managing up.

I'm not asked questions or challenged.

There is no vehicle for those who are managed to discuss how they are managed—it's to do with insecurity.

It's difficult to criticize your line manager.

Reflexive inquiry: insight, critique and transformation

To facilitate the development from *insight* and *critique* to *transformation* I needed to speak from a consultancy position about the research process and engage the leadership group in a dialogue of learning and development. A 4D cycle process was used to structure the dialogue. However, unlike an AI, where the frame is set for *valuation* (what works well, affirmative talk, highlights from experience), the frame offered here was that of *reflexive evaluation* and *learning*.[1] An important context set was that my presentation of themes represented a partial picture. However, I pointed out that mine was not the only partial picture. I proposed the task of building a picture together, using the material and themes from the interviews as a base from which to explore and identify areas for management development. I presented the tool of the *strange loop*. I had been told that the group loved diagrams and models so I was hoping to be participating in an unfamiliar but stimulating language game.

What follows is the design of the structure for dialogue:

The 4D cycle process

Discovery: learning from experience

In four groups of three or four

- take one loop and connect it with experience;
- discuss an episode of management communication that fits the loop and one that does not;
- amend the loop to fit your experience;

- think about how the contextual stories would need to change so they would construct discursive invitation rather than discursive closure;
- present to group.

My reflections

I observed that in general the analysis was felt to be fitting and provided a frame for people coming from different positions and interests in an intercultural context to identify points of connection, disconnection, and development. I was impressed by the constructive honesty and creativity in the group in grappling with sensitive communication and functional and structural issues as people worked on the patterns that had been presented.

The word *disconnection* had a powerful presence. Participants acknowledged the level of fragmentation of their working lives and expressed the desire for a new kind of relationship. The word *management* became a focus, with some desire expressed to *get rid of* the word altogether! For me, that represented a (defensive) "red herring" and yet another example of discursive closure, constraining a shared dialogue about management as an honourable and necessary practice. A pivotal moment was when the CEO spoke of his ambivalence about being a manager. He was given feedback that the organization needed him to be a manager and that speaking about himself in that way created constraint. I saw this as a complex message to the CEO, but ultimately acknowledging and supporting his power and ability and comprising a message from the group to the group about the need for taking greater responsibility for how organizational identities, relationships, and cultures were represented.

Dream: developing purpose, role and function of managers

In same groups

- take one of three positions—inquirer, listener, and speaker;
- inquire into potential effective role and relational responsibilities, expectations, connections, and boundaries in the individual's management context;

- after thirty minutes, inquirer and listener reflect in front of speaker on what they have heard then return to speaker for five minutes;
- layered reflection from each position in large group;
- back in small groups work on defining core principles and practices of management role on flip chart;
- present to group;
- create agreement on core principles and practices.

My reflections

I observed that the structure encouraged people to speak about their experience and have their experience heard. Out of the reflection, groups prepared presentations on core principles and practices of management. It was interesting that there was a lot of overlap in the presentations and unexpected high levels of agreement. This process suggested to me the value of meaning-making in this way for both its content and its process. However, there was quite a high level of concern in the group that we would be unable to create more concrete commitments and plans by the end of the two days. This suggested to me that attention may need to be given to the ways meetings are coordinated so that contexts, purposes, parameters, and rules for involvement are clear and sustained in a process of meeting. It also suggested that there may not be sufficient mechanisms for shared approaches to *instrumental reasoning* in the organization. A fear was being expressed that meaning-making could function as an end in itself.

Design: improving organizational and individual competencies

Working alone

- identify actions that you and others should take to improve management/staff patterns and practices and write proposals down, with name, one on each paper;
- negotiation of proposals—turn-taking round the table— proposals accepted unless challenged;
- agreements created about how process/decisions are communicated to staff.

My reflections

I observed that many grounded proposals were made, discussed with care and respect, and accepted. The proposals made were linked to the analysis and the discussion that took place over the two days. I observed that risks were taken in the claims made about what was important and meaningful. There were areas that could not be agreed, as might be expected.

Deconstruction: communication, learning and critique

- Small group inquiry.
- How did the communication process show strength and fragility of management discourses and practices?
- What part did the individual play in contributing to strength and fragility?
- What is the learning from this about management processes?
- Share in large group.

My reflections

I observed that:

- the group responded to clear, purposeful leadership
- the purposes of all participants were incorporated and coordinated, facilitating ownership
- difficult sensitive areas were enabled to be discussed through providing clear structures and focused content
- a strong desire was shown for greater connection and coherence between the parts and the whole of the organization, with appropriate concern expressed for how that could be achieved, while recognizing this needed care and attention by all.

Discussion

While there are many potential variations for an RI repertoire, I have attempted to show with one case how RI can work in practice, through connecting a research phase and a consultancy phase of a piece of work. In returning to the five principles we can reflect on its impact.

Systemic principle

The leadership of the organization had understood that they were participating in unwanted patterns. However, they were unable to create a vocabulary for their articulation or for new action. In offering the strange loop as a frame for the themes of discursive closure and invitation that were of most concern, a systemic evaluation could be made that provided patterns of connection out of an experience of fragmentation.

Individuals and the group were able to see and explore how their actions contributed to the whole and began to create new stories that were more effectively connected to their (emerging) purposes, for instance, a decision was made about the need for a management code of practice.

Constructionist principle

The potential for greater coherence was facilitated through these new narratives of identity, relationship, and culture. In creating the conditions for dialogue about the contexts shaping the unwanted looped patterns, leverage was created for new stories of obligation and entitlement. From the perspective of person position it became clear that the notions of *I* as a manager and *we* as managers were undermined in this organization. There was deep ambivalence about the adoption of management identity from the CEO "down". When faced with this anomaly, it was understood that a greater leadership *agency* needed to be developed for the sake of the survival of the organization, those who worked in it and those it worked for. In the context of reflexive evaluation, the moral logic and confusion in people's behaviour came into focus. For instance, on examining the contexts shaping the loops, it could be both understood and problematized why everyone, whether working in the field or in the senior management team, protected their own territory and experienced outside demands as an interference.

Critical principle

When faced with the impact of the connection between shared patterns lived and stories told, critical consciousness became a force for challenge and change. A greater awareness was facilitated about the costs and benefits of change and no change and perceptions of interest began to change. People were able to speak explicitly about their perceptions of their own sectional interests and how these perceptions shaped behaviour and created constraining patterns. By positioning all participants as contributing to the looped patterns, second and third order critique was achieved. Reflection occurred about feelings of pressure and patterned ways of interpreting and acting in relation to such pressures.

Appreciative principle

It was of great value for this group of leaders to achieve a shared sense of vulnerability and strength as individuals and group through this process of evaluation, set not in a context of truth and blame claims but in a context of building a picture of the workings of communication. The notions of *positive* and *negative* were not relevant in this discourse. Participants developed an emergent appreciation of the choices that were and could be made and their consequences for discursive invitation and closure. For instance, people made commitments to attend strategic meetings that had previously been avoided, out of a realization that non-attendance created unwanted communication, identities, relationships, and culture.

Complexity principle

The strange loop tool worked as a catalyst for insight, critique, and transformation. Through the connection of polarized feeling, meaning, and action into a coherent narrative that made (moral) sense, participants were newly able to coordinate feeling, meaning, and action with agency and purpose, less constrained by constraining discourses.

Summary

Part III has explored the potential place of research in a consultancy process to assist in reflexive evaluation of the organization by the organization. It has shown how the identification of a phase of the work as research can facilitate a process of insight, critique, and transformation in the context of RI. It is important to underline how such a process can be both liberating and fragile, holding the potential for both transformation and the reinforcement of unwanted patterns. The reflexive positioning of the consultant researcher is integral to an effective process. There is a need for clarity about which context is created at any one time and the entitlements and obligations that are meaningful in that context to be clear and agreed. It needs to be understood that all participants, including the consultant researcher, are to cultivate a position of second and third order critique and learning and be open to patterns of discursive closure and invitation. Finally, it is important that the inquiry is conducted with a spirit of openness, humility, and learning, with the hope that such a spirit is communicated and adopted as a discourse that shapes future patterns.

Note

1. "Deconstruction" became the fourth D, differing from the AI structure where the fourth D is "delivery".

PART IV

CONCLUSIONS AND DEVELOPMENTS

CHAPTER SEVEN

Reflexive strategies for critical consciousness

T he work thus far has offered a theoretical frame for consultancy, constructing broad principles out of different but
connected theoretical traditions, brought alive in various
ways through case illustrations. The model is intended to provide
both sufficient structure and flexibility, that the form of its practices
be coherent, but the detail, always situationally specific, requiring
creative attunement to the contextual considerations at hand. I hope
the model provides the possibility of holding the complexity of
consultancy life, while encouraging the making of reflexive choices
and priorities in action. The positioning of reflexivity as the context
giving core meaning to consultancy action inevitably creates discursive closure of some possibilities while inviting others. For instance,
the argument as it is developed here connects poor reflexivity to
strategies of polarization and fragmentation and discourages such
strategies where there is insufficient consideration of their systemic
effects. Such strategies may or may not be within our consciousness. The argument is thus made for the development of critical
consciousness about patterns of feeling, meaning, and action so that
our communication does not do *ecological* damage. In this spirit,
I have become preoccupied with the form our fragmented and

polarized products of communication can take and with reflexive strategies for their development.

In a recent book (Oliver, Herasymowych, & Senko, 2003), reflexive practice has been specifically connected to the handling of complexity and to the problem of polarization. The tool of the looped pattern for facilitating the management of reflexive action is the subject of the book. Characteristic forms of loop are offered as typical patterns within organizational life. Here, as I end this book, I present and develop that work, appreciating that it represents an attempt to identify patterns that repeat, in a sense, patterns of patterns, but also appreciating that its scope has been limited. The work connects each loop to an experience of anxiety, or challenge to our own patterns lived and stories told at cultural, relational, and identity levels. It is proposed that the relationship we take to anxiety and the ways we manage the anxiety felt by selves and others is a legitimate and productive concern in organizational life and organizational consultancy. The form the loop takes will depend on our relationship to the challenge presented. The patterns offered are representative of typical patterns but do not pretend to cover all experience. However, they offer a structure and content that can facilitate and stimulate other possibilities.

Oliver, Herasymowych, and Senko (2003) propose the *charmed loop*[1] as representative of a circular process of feeling, meaning, and action, incorporating reflexivity and enabling learning. The *hexed loop*, on the other hand, is a vicious circle that shows poor reflexivity. Both patterns show predictability in their trajectory and do not use the strategy of polarization to manage the complexity of communication. The charmed loop works to hold complexity; the hexed loop fragments and splits off experience so it only allows connection to the pessimistic and a story of threat, but stays in that reality of mistrust and *paranoia*; hope doesn't surface. The strange loop, as we have seen, represents an oscillating and polarized pattern between hexed and charmed loops, optimism and pessimism, invitation and closure and creates ripple effects so that others are invited or pressured into their own strange loop patterns. Figures 22–28 illustrate these representations and offer examples of strange loop, highlighting the attempt of the strange loop to manage the pressure and anxiety of complexity and show, in abstract form, some of the patterned by-products of our relationship to anxiety. Each loop

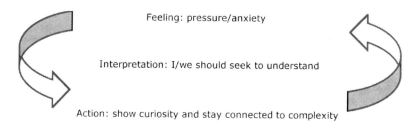

Figure 22.   Charmed loop

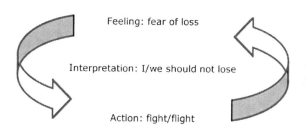

Figure 23.   Hexed loop

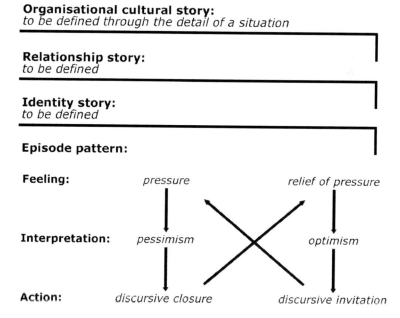

Figure 24.   A reminder of the basic template for strange loop pattern

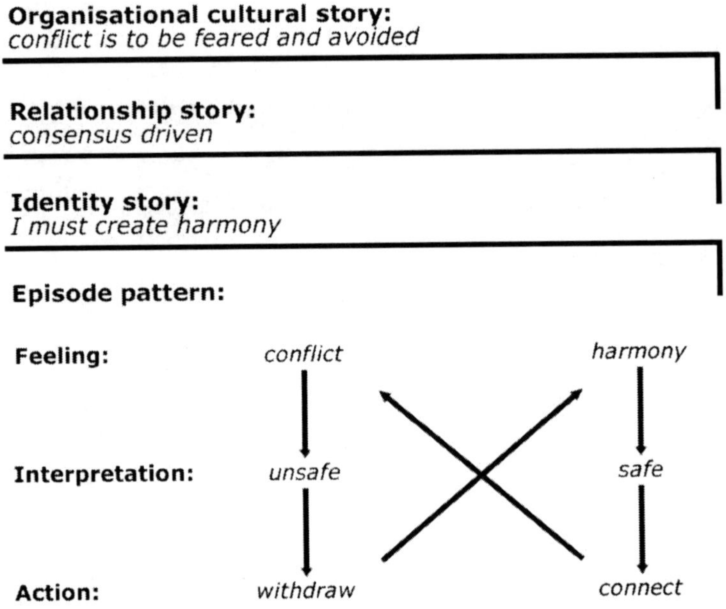

Organisational cultural story:
conflict is to be feared and avoided

Relationship story:
consensus driven

Identity story:
I must create harmony

Episode pattern:

Feeling:	conflict	harmony
Interpretation:	unsafe	safe
Action:	withdraw	connect

Figure 25. Pseudo charmed loop

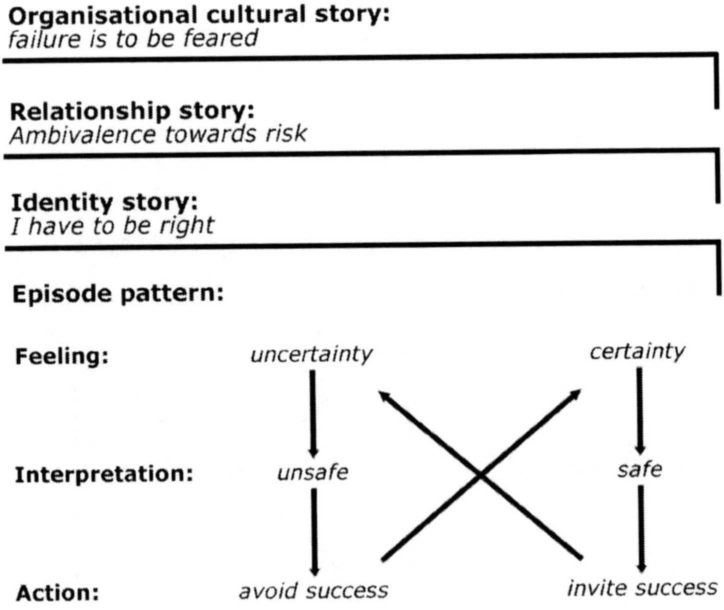

Organisational cultural story:
failure is to be feared

Relationship story:
Ambivalence towards risk

Identity story:
I have to be right

Episode pattern:

Feeling:	uncertainty	certainty
Interpretation:	unsafe	safe
Action:	avoid success	invite success

Figure 26. Pseudo hexed loop

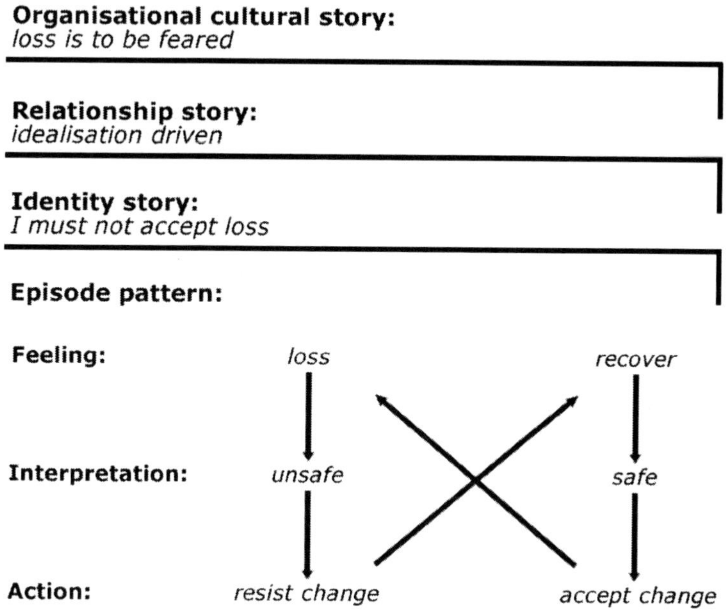

Organisational cultural story:
loss is to be feared

Relationship story:
idealisation driven

Identity story:
I must not accept loss

Episode pattern:

Feeling: loss   recover

Interpretation: unsafe   safe

Action: resist change   accept change

Figure 27. Lost charmed loop

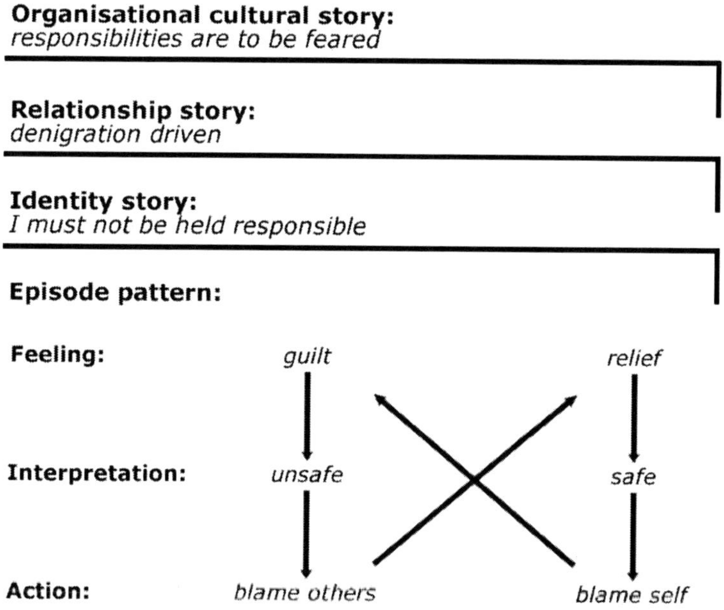

Organisational cultural story:
responsibilities are to be feared

Relationship story:
denigration driven

Identity story:
I must not be held responsible

Episode pattern:

Feeling: guilt   relief

Interpretation: unsafe   safe

Action: blame others   blame self

Figure 28. Lost hexed loop

provides a polarized strategy to a problem of anxiety and shows oscillating pessimism and optimism, closed and open behaviours (summarized in Table 5). Whatever the temporary position taken up, as episodes oscillate from one state to another there is no stability and no possibility for coherence until the narrative of the pattern is created. These pre-patterns can facilitate hypothesizing, particularly in a context where anxiety and fear are evident and there feels no stability to the lived pattern. Once patterns have been identified, strategies for discursive invitation can be developed (Oliver, Herasymowych, & Senko, 2003).

Table 6 shows different levels and stages of strategy in the face of strange loops. It is not assumed that once a strange loop is identified, it is necessary to change behaviour. However, the development of consciousness that grows from connecting patterns of feeling, meaning, and action to contextual stories in this way will have its own undetermined consequences.

Table 5   Summary of charmed and hexed strange loop patterns

Loop	Relationship to anxiety	Feeling	Distortion of meaning	Closed action
Pseudo charmed	Flight/connect	Anxiety about conflict	Optimism	Avoid conflict
Pseudo hexed	Flight/connect	Anxiety about failure	Pessimism	Avoid success
Lost charmed	Fight/ capitulate	Anxiety about loss	Idealization	Resist change
Lost hexed	Fight/ capitulate	Anxiety about responsibility	Denigration	Blame others

Table 6. Levels of reflexive strategy

Strategy	Action	Benefit	Vulnerability
Continue the pattern	Taking responsibility for one's part in contributing to the pattern and for its effects.	Increased consciousness of systemic connections and choices.	No change
Examine the pattern	Taking responsibility for one's part in the pattern and examining it in depth before taking action.	Widening context; seeing how patterns lived and stories told connect. Potential for reflexive choice.	No change
Accept and live in the relationship	No change to content of contextual stories and consequences for pattern but relationship changes to acceptance.	Relationship to pattern changes; it loses its power. First/second order change.	Being drawn back in.
Exit the relationship	Change of relationship to contextual stories and/or change to pattern of behaviour.	Clarity of need for change created and acted upon. First/second order change.	New situation/old loop
Create a charmed loop	Critical appreciation of what this new reflexive positioning to patterns lived and stories told might create.	Potential for first, second and third order change with this reflexive consciousness.	Complacency
Sustain a charmed loop	Experiment with ways of being and challenge stories told and patterns lived.	First, second and third order change become habitual.	Living at the edge of chaos

Summary

I hope this last chapter has shown the potential of structuring empirical material, for consultancy–research purposes by imagining links between feeling, meaning, and action and their contexts in the form of characteristic fight or flight loops in the face of anxiety and complexity. This work is evolving.

For the practising consultant, the ideas offered here might, at times, appear academically dense and the practice contexts may appear privileged and inaccessible. It is tempting to try to distil what is proposed into manageable bites but also tempting not to! The reflexive principles and practices offered here, can, I believe, with modification, be used in any social context. If I were invited to articulate a modified representation of RI, I think I would say the following.

In any exchange with and in organizations, think about the contexts you (and/or they) are acting out of and into, and consider whether your (and/or their) responses are sufficiently fitting to satisfy your emerging purposes. Dialogue processes can be designed to enhance coherence but we always need to be alert to the situational requirements of the complex moment.

Note

1. This definition of charmed loop differs from Cronen, Johnson, and Lannaman (1982).

REFERENCES

Alvesson, M. (2003). Beyond neopositivists, romantics and localists: a reflexive approach to interviews in organisational research. *Academy Management Review, 28*(1): 13–33.

Alvesson, M., & Deetz, S. (2000). *Doing Critical Management Research.* London: Sage.

Alvesson, M., & Skoldberg, K. (2000). *Reflexive Methodology.* London: Sage.

Andersen, T. (1987), Reflecting teams: dialogue and meta-dialogue in clinical work. *Family Process, 26*(4): 415–428.

Anderson, H., Cooperrider, D., Gergen, K. J., Gergen, M., McNamee, S., & Whitney, D. (2001). *The Appreciative Organization.* Taos, New Mexico: Taos Institute.

Asch, S. (1952). *Social Psychology.* Englewood Cliffs, NJ.

Barge, J. K., & Oliver, C. (2003). Working with appreciation in managerial practice. *Academy of Management Review, 28*(1): 124–142.

Bateson, G. (1972). *Steps to an Ecology of Mind.* New York: Ballantine.

Bion, W. R. (1959). *Experiences in Groups and Other Papers.* New York: Basic Books.

Boscolo, L., Cecchin, G., Hoffman, L., & Penn, P. (1987). *Milan Systemic Family Therapy.* New York: Basic Books.

Buber, M. (1970). *I and Thou*. New York: Simon & Schuster.

Burr, V. (1995). *An Introduction to Social Constructionism*. London: Routledge.

Campbell, D. (2000). *The Socially Constructed Organization*. London: Karnac.

Cooperrider, D. L. (1998). What is appreciative inquiry? In: S. A. Hammond & C. Royal (Eds.), *Lessons from the Field: Applying Appreciative Inquiry*. Plano, TX: Practical Press.

Cooperrider, D. L., & Whitney, D. (1999). *Appreciative Inquiry*. San Francisco: Berrett-Koehler.

Cronen, V., & Pearce, W. B. (1985). Toward an explanation of how the Milan method works. In: D. Campbell & R. Draper (Eds.), *Applications of Systemic Therapy* (pp. 69–84). London: Grune and Stratton.

Cronen, V., Johnson, K., & Lannaman, J. (1982). Paradoxes, double binds and reflexive loops: an alternative theoretical perspective. *Family Process, 21*: 91–112.

De Bono, E. (2003). *Why So Stupid*. Dublin: Blackhall.

Elkjaer, B. (2001). The learning organisation: an undelivered promise. *Management Learning, 32*(4): 437–452.

Emery, M., & Purser, R. (1996). *The Search Conference: A Powerful Method for Planning Organizational Change and Community Action*. San Fancisco: Jossey-Bass.

Eve, R. A., Horsfall, S., & Lee, M. E. (1997). *Chaos, Complexity and Sociology*. London: Sage.

Gergen, K. J. (1989). *Texts of Identity*. London: Sage.

Habermas, J. (1970). Knowledge and interest. In: D. Emmet & A. MacIntyre (Eds.), *Sociological Theory and Philosophical Analysis* (pp. 36–54). London: Macmillan.

Habermas, J. (1984). *The Theory of Communicative Action, Vol. 1: Reason and the Rationalisation of Society*. Boston, MA: Beacon.

Hammond, S. A. (1998). *The Thin Book of Appreciative Inquiry* (2nd edn). Plano, TX: Thin Book.

Harre, R., & Langenhove, L. (1999). *Positioning Theory*. Oxford: Blackwell.

Kolb, D. (1984). *Experiential Learning*. Englewood Cliffs, NJ: Prentice Hall.

Lang, W. P., Little, M., & Cronen, V. (1990). The systemic professional: domains of action and the question of neutrality. *Human Systems, 1*(1): 39–56.

Lave, J., & Wenger, E. (1991). *Situated Learning: Legitimate Peripheral Participation*. Cambridge: Cambridge University Press.

Maturana, H. R., & Varela, F. J. (1987). *The Tree of Knowledge: The Biological Roots of Human Understanding*. Boston: New Science Library.

Oliver, C. (1992). A focus on moral story making in therapy using co-ordinated management of meaning (CMM). *Human Systems, 3*: 217–231.

Oliver, C. (1996) Systemic eloquence. *Human Systems, 7*(4).

Oliver, C. (2005). Critical appreciative inquiry: reworking a consultancy discourse. In: E. Peck (Ed.), *Organisational Development in Healthcare*. Oxford: Radcliffe.

Oliver, C., & Barge, J. K. (2002). Appreciative inquiry as aesthetic sensi-tivity: co-ordination of meaning, purpose and reflexivity. In: C. Dalsgaard, T. Meisner, & K Voetman (Eds.), *Change: Appreciative Conversations in Theory and Practice*. Denmark: Psykologisk Forlag.

Oliver, C., & Brittain, G. (2001). Situated knowledge management. *Career Development International, 6*(7): 403–413.

Oliver, C., & Lang, S. (1994). Managing difficult people. *Managing: in Local Government and Education*. Nov/Dec issue.

Oliver, C., Herasymowych, M., & Senko, H. (2003). *Complexity, Relationships and Strange Loops: Reflexive Practice Guide*. Calgary, Canada: MHA Institute.

Pearce, W. B. (1989). *Communication and the Human Condition*. Carbon-dale, ILL: Southern Illinois University Press.

Pearce, W. B. (1994). *Interpersonal Communication: Making Social Worlds*. New York: Harper Collins.

Peck, E. (2005). *Organisational Development in Healthcare*. Oxford: Radcliffe.

Penn, P. (1985). Feed forward: future questions, future maps. *Family Process, 24*: 299–311.

Raelin, J. A. (2001). Public reflection as the basis of learning. *Management Learning, 32*(1): 11–30.

Ryan, F. (2004). The future conference: does it have potential as an action research method? In: C. Cassells & G. Symon (Eds.), *Qualitative Methods of Organizational Research*. London: Sage.

Selvini, M., Cecchin, G., Prata, J., & Boscolo, L. (1978). *Paradox and Counterparadox*. New York: Jason Aronson.

Senge, P. (1990). *The Fifth Discipline*. New York: Doubleday.

Silverman, D. (2000). *Doing Qualitative Research: A Practical Handbook*. London, Sage.

Shotter, J. (1993). *Conversational Realities*. London: Sage.

Stacey, R. D. (2000) Complexity at the edge of the basic assumption group in L. Gould, L. F. Stapley, & M. Stein (Eds.), *The Systems Dynamics of Organizations*. London: Karnac.

Stacey, R. D., Griffin, D., & Shaw, P. (2000). *Complexity and Management: Fad or Radical Challenge To Systems Thinking?* London: Routledge.

Tomm, K. (1985). Circular interviewing: A multifaceted clinical tool. In: D. Campbell & R. Draper (Eds.), *Applications of Systemic Family Therapy: The Milan Method* (pp. 33–45). New York: Grune and Stratton.

Wilmott, H. (1993). Strength is ignorance; slavery is freedom: managing culture in modern organizations. *Journal of Management Studies, 30*(4): 515–552.

Wittgenstein, L. (1953). *Philosophical Investigations* G. Anscombe (Trans.). New York: Macmillan.

INDEX

9 781855 753587